Ope

Firstly I would like to thank the artists who applied to 'Open Cube', and particularly the 38 who attended the interview in London, including those who participated in the exhibition: Matt Ager, Adriano Amaral, Frank Ammerlaan, Helen Barff, Sarah Bernhardt, Martin John Callanan, Nuno Direitinho, Venisha Francis-Hinkson, Rodrigo Garcia Dutra, Rowena Harris, Alan Magee, Fay Nicolson, Daniel de Paula, Nada Prlja, Nicky Teegan, Jacopo Trabona and Caitlin Yardley.

I am especially grateful to Jay Jopling and Susan May, who supported this experiment, as well as Lewis Gilbert, Hannah Gruy and Susannah Hyman, who endured with me through the process of sorting through the applications and interviews, and for putting together the exhibition. I would also like to thank the wonderful White Cube installation team of James Balmer, Mauro Bonacina, Harry Burry, Matthew McQuillan, Darren Norman, Melv Thomas and Carina Thoren; and Robin Kirsten and Honey Luard, who edited this publication – allowing us to include so many interviews and images of the show – and my assistant in São Paulo, Isabella Rjelli.

Thanks also to Pablo León de la Barra, for his critiques and comments on this project and others, and for Rivane Neuenschwander and Jochen Volz for their friendly support in London.

Adriano Pedrosa

Contents

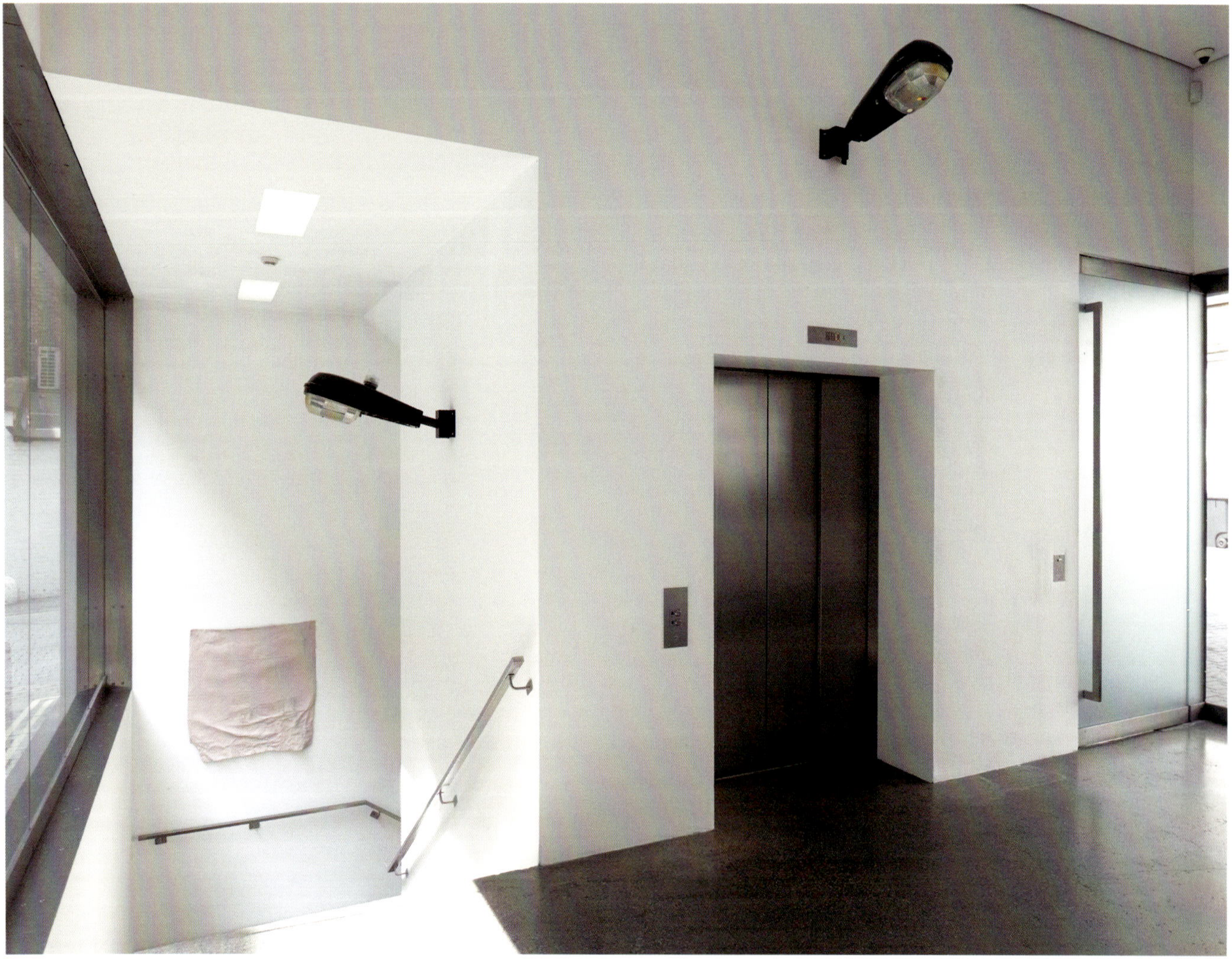

In conversation

Pablo León de la Barra interviews Adriano Pedrosa

Pablo León de la Barra: Last time I saw you was in March in Sharjah, where you told me about the exhibition you were curating at White Cube. I reacted by being critical and saying, 'Adriano, you don't need to do an exhibition in a commercial gallery'; I couldn't understand why a serious curator like you who curated the 2011 Istanbul Biennial, and who has been part of the curatorial teams of the São Paulo Biennial in 1998 and 2006, would need to engage with one of the biggest and most commercial galleries in London. So my first question would be: why did you accept to do this exhibition and how and why are you attempting to turn around the rules of the game?
Adriano Pedrosa: It was after our meeting in Sharjah that I felt it could be interesting to have this conversation, and I also wanted to submit myself to the same interviewing process to which I submitted the artists. I did think very carefully about how I could turn the invitation to curate an exhibition at White Cube into a project that was more experimental, investigative, and how that could somehow challenge the usual parameters and processes in a project involving one of the most prestigious commercial galleries in London, if not in the world. Perhaps what was expected of me as a Brazilian curator, and given that the gallery had just opened a space in São Paulo, was that I would bring with me established and prestigious artists from Brazil, Latin America and elsewhere, thus relying on my own previous research, connections and archive, and this was something that I wanted to turn around.
In fact, initially I had thought of a more traditional thematic group exhibition, but then I realised that I needed to take advantage of the opportunity that was offered to me to somehow undo this expectation,

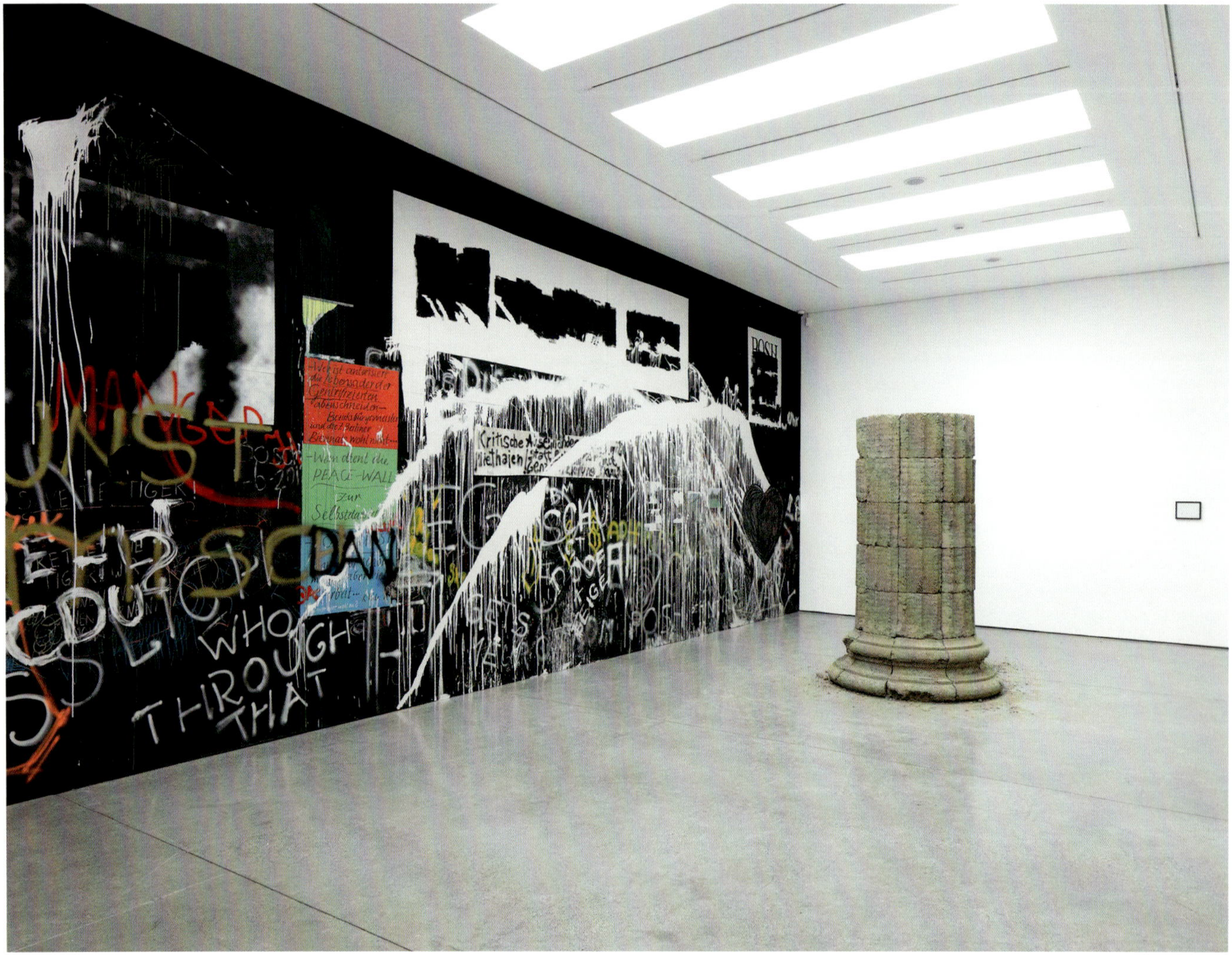
POSH
Kritische
Miethajen
PEACE-WALL
DAN
WHO
THROUGH
THAT

opening up new research for myself as well as for the gallery. This is how I came to propose 'Open Cube', which plays on the gallery's name, and is essentially an open call exhibition, something that is the opposite of what a prestigious gallery working with established, blue-chip artists would ever do.

After starting to review the 2,900 applications that we received, I decided to radicalise this and interview only artists who I had never worked with, and in fact only those who I had never heard of. I am interested in pushing the parameters and the limits of the space, project or institution that I am working in. For example, at 'Panorama da Arte Brasileira' (Museu de Arte Moderna de São Paulo, 2009), a biennial of Brazilian artists, I selected only foreigners who somehow worked with Brazilian themes, therefore proposing a new understanding of what Brazilian art is, one that is not necessarily made by a Brazilian, but has Brazilian content. In the interviews for 'Open Cube' I was interested in learning from the artists what their thoughts were on the gallery, and the first question I asked them was why they had applied and what their perception of the gallery was. Above all, an exhibition at White Cube is a tremendous opportunity for many artists, particularly younger ones or those without representation, and my invitation and curatorial proposal attempted to turn over this opportunity to them, even if only for a small number of them because of space constraints. I come from an artist's background – I was a young artist once without opportunities to show my work (though I have since stopped making art) – so I wanted to take advantage of this great exhibition space, the generous resources and the wonderful team that White Cube made available to me, and to offer it to these artists.

It is interesting that the expectation to curate a Brazilian or Latin American or International exhibition morphed into what is mostly a local show, in which the majority of the artists are either studying or have recently graduated. I was looking to do away with the usual process of selection for exhibitions, such as relying on one's own archives, knowledge and colleagues, instead proposing a democratic process by which artists could apply, and that is why we launched the open call in January 2013 on Art Agenda. Anyone could apply, one of the conditions was that they needed to be available for an interview with me in London in March. I had also recently worked on the 12th

Istanbul Biennial, in 2011, where there had been an open call component. Although only a fraction of artists in the biennial were selected through that process, I was still very much impressed with the material we received. An open call was something particularly interesting in a city like London, which is quite open to foreign students, and has so many great art schools.

I strongly believe that as a curator we work above all for the artists, to present them in the best possible way, giving them support to develop their work, and of course not forgetting the responsibility towards the public and the institution. As curators we have the privilege of choosing the artists we work with, who remain our priority. In this sense 'Open Cube' was essentially an exhibition for the artists. The play on 'White Cube', both in terms of Brian O'Doherty's renowned series of essays published collectively as *Inside the White Cube: The Ideology of the Gallery Space*, which first appeared in *Artforum* in 1976, as well as being the name of the gallery, offered further possibilities. So in many ways with 'Open Cube' there was an attempt to transform the dense, opaque, somewhat impenetrable white cube, into an open, democratic, transparent cube, both in terms of the open call format, as well as through the recording of the interviews, which were done with the artists' consent and then transcribed, with passages from these published in this catalogue.

The extraordinary number of applications we received was a testament to how valuable this opportunity was for so many artists, and I have since been told that White Cube Mason's Yard has never had so many people at an opening. Furthermore, we have put together a substantial publication, and I believe this will be these artists' most important catalogue to date. It will be interesting to see in 5 or 10 years time what has happened to these artists.

In the curator's world there seems to be some kind of unspoken ethic where most of the time it is viewed negatively when a curator engages with the commercial side of the art world. You yourself have always accepted the reality of the commercial aspect of art, and curate two private collections, one in Lisbon and another in São Paulo, and have curated in galleries and art fairs like 'Zona Maco Sur', Mexico (2009–11); 'SP-Arte', São Paulo and 'Frieze Masters', London (2012–13). How do you deal with your relationship to the commercial art world without everything becoming incestuous?

Announcement in Art Agenda for 'Open Cube', January 2013

White Cube

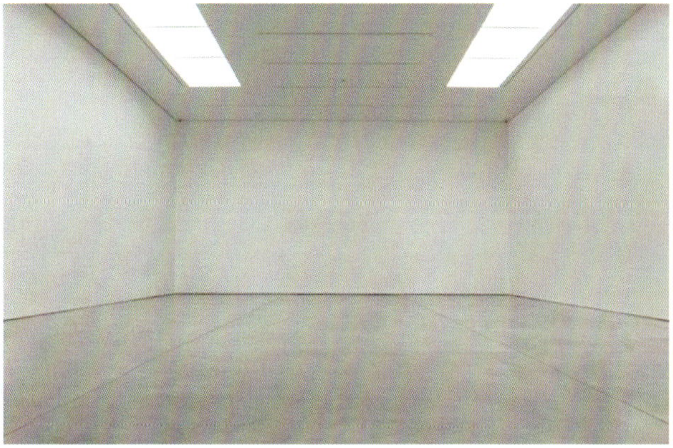

White Cube Mason's Yard, Courtesy White Cube.

Call for entries: Open Cube

Curated by Adriano Pedrosa, White Cube Mason's Yard, London 2013

Application deadline: 28 February 2013

White Cube Mason's Yard
25–26 Mason's Yard
London SW1Y 6BU

www.whitecube.com/submission

Share

Leading contemporary art gallery White Cube has invited São Paulo-based curator Adriano Pedrosa to curate an exhibition at their Mason's Yard gallery, London, in July 2013. Pedrosa's project, titled *Open Cube*, will attempt to infiltrate the hierarchies of the gallery system by inviting any interested artists to submit works to be included in the exhibition. By opening up the selection process, Pedrosa wishes to unsettle the system of gallery practices, initiating a dialogue with artists that might not have access to this network.

Shortlisted artists must be available for interviews in London with Adriano Pedrosa in March and April.

A comprehensive catalogue with texts by Pedrosa will accompany the exhibition.

Adriano Pedrosa is an independent curator, editor, and writer currently based in São Paulo. He has curated numerous international exhibitions and was adjunct curator of the 24th Bienal de São Paulo (1998, with chief curator Paulo Herkenhoff), co-curator of the 27th Bienal de São Paulo (2006, with chief curator Lisette Lagnado) and co-curator of the 12th Istanbul Biennial (2011, with Jens Hoffmann). He has published extensively on contemporary art in numerous catalogues and magazines, and is the founding director of PIESP—Programa Independente da Escola São Paulo.

Full details on how to apply are available at www.whitecube.com/submission.

MORE FROM WHITE CUBE

White Cube announces editions by Marc Quinn, Cerith Wyn Evans and Eberhard Havekost

Cerith Wyn Evans at White Cube Mason's Yard

I am an independent curator without any institutional affiliations, which is why I can do these projects with galleries, fairs, collections, as well as museums and biennials. That is probably because I live in Brazil, where there are very few opportunities for a curator to work full-time in an institution with independence, autonomy and support. Perhaps things are changing now, with museums developing stronger programmes, but for a very long time in Brazil it was the galleries who were doing the more international and experimental programmes. This is also true in other scenes outside Europe and America. This unspoken ethic that you describe comes from a Eurocentric perspective that cannot be applied to the rest of the world, as we have learned from other fields and disciplines. In fact it is noteworthy to see how many of the Latin American curators from our generation have curated for galleries and art fairs, for example Julieta González, José Roca, Rodrigo Moura, María Inés Rodrígues, Juan Gaitán and yourself; perhaps my own work has helped open this up. I have chosen to remain independent because I have been able to develop more interesting projects this way, as I do not have to deal with the demanding institutional bureaucracies of the day-to-day activities of full-time museum curators. But as an independent curator I have also felt that it was important to try to bridge the commercial and institutional worlds.

We have seen how art fairs, for example, have had an increasing presence in the art world, yet very few spaces in an art fair are in fact curated, as there is by and large a prevalence of market forces there. So when I am asked to develop projects for fairs, I am always thinking about how I can push the boundaries, how I can create spaces that are more critical and investigative, to somehow occupy sections of the art fair curatorially. At the Mexico art fair 'Zona Maco', this meant creating the project room section for solo presentations by artists from the Global South, or those who were somehow engaging with the Global South, which is why I titled it 'Zona Maco Sur' – *sur* meaning south in Spanish. That project made sense there because it seemed to me that Mexican curators and collectors are often excessively turned towards the United States and Europe. After the third edition in 2011, which included only female artists and consolidated the section with the support of the director Zélika García, I thought it was time to pass the position over to another curator; Patrick Charpenel in 2012, and then Juan Gaitán in

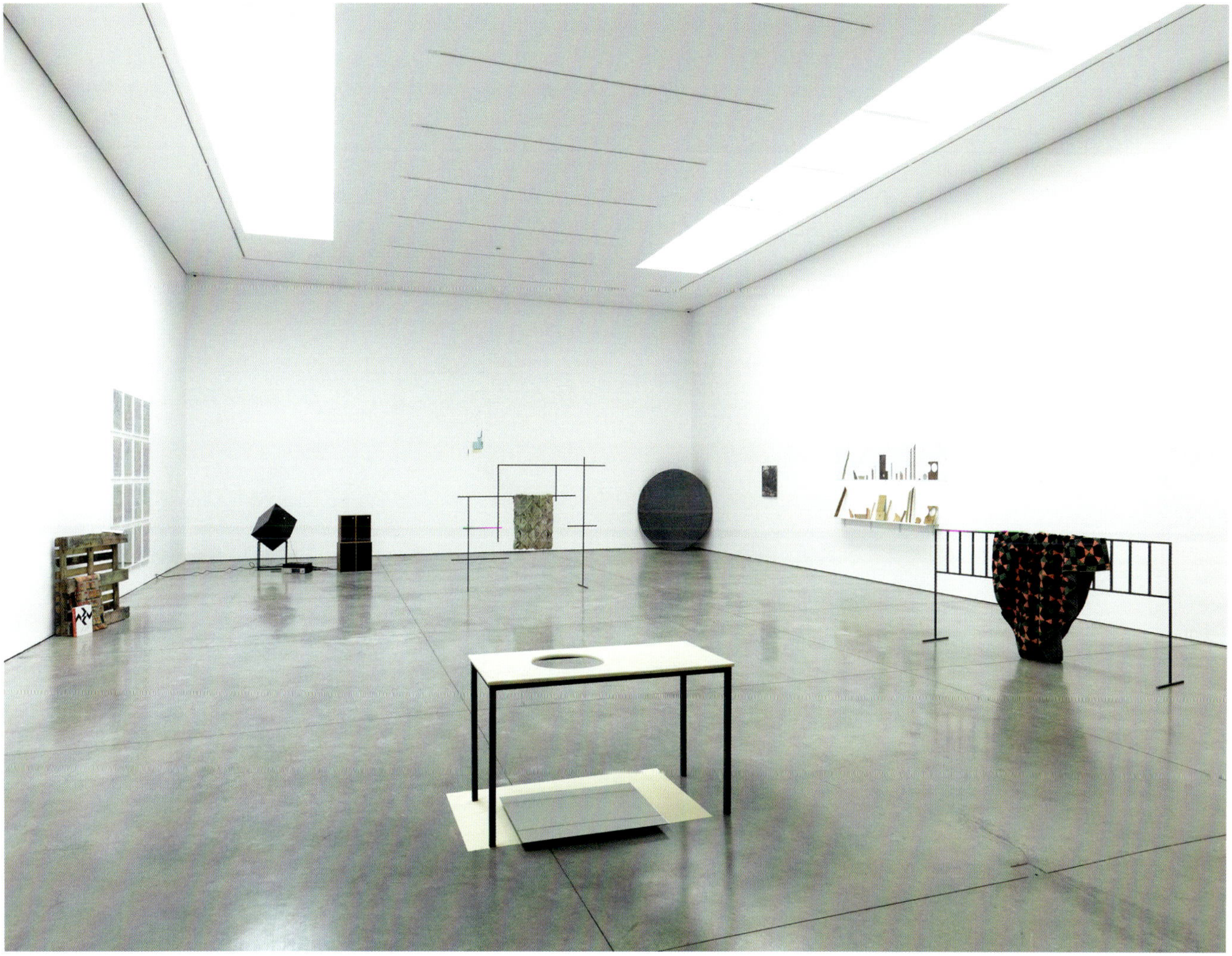

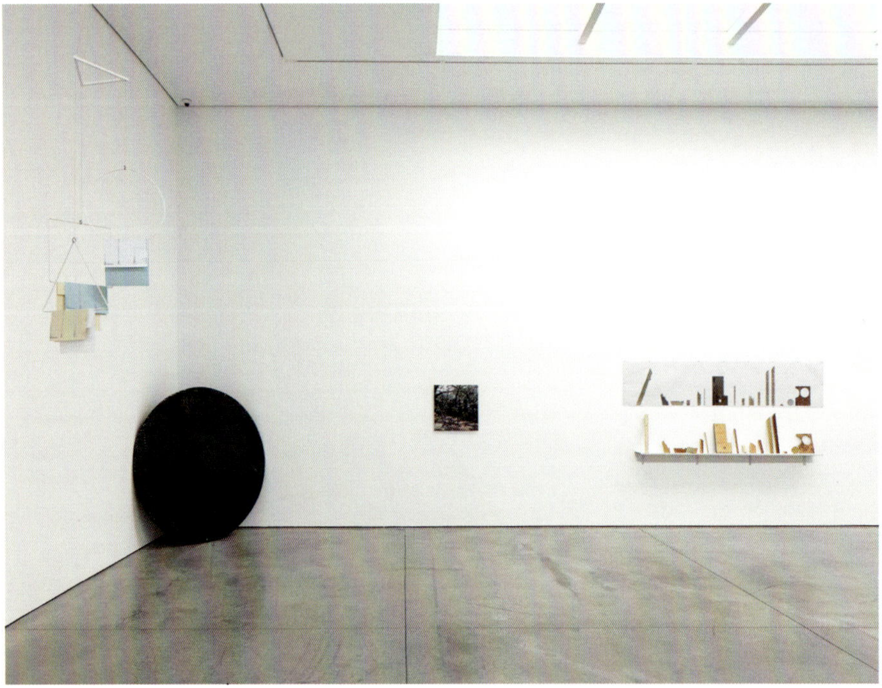

2013. At 'Frieze Masters' the 'Spotlight' section is dedicated to the monographic presentation of 20th Century Masters, and I've been advancing a more experimental, challenging and diverse notion of the Master, bringing in conceptualist practices with a strong presence of female artists and artists working outside of Europe and America, though not excluding these artists. At 'SP-Arte' in São Paulo I was invited to create a project for the fair, and instead of a project room section I proposed 'Laboratório Curatorial', which selects four young curators to submit proposals for small group shows to be developed over a six month period, in conversation with myself and other curators. They also have an open call and I conduct interviews with the curators to select the projects that will be developed. In the end the young curators also receive funding to travel to see an exhibition such as 'dOCUMENTA', or the Venice or Istanbul biennials.

The issue of incestuousness is an interesting one. In our profession

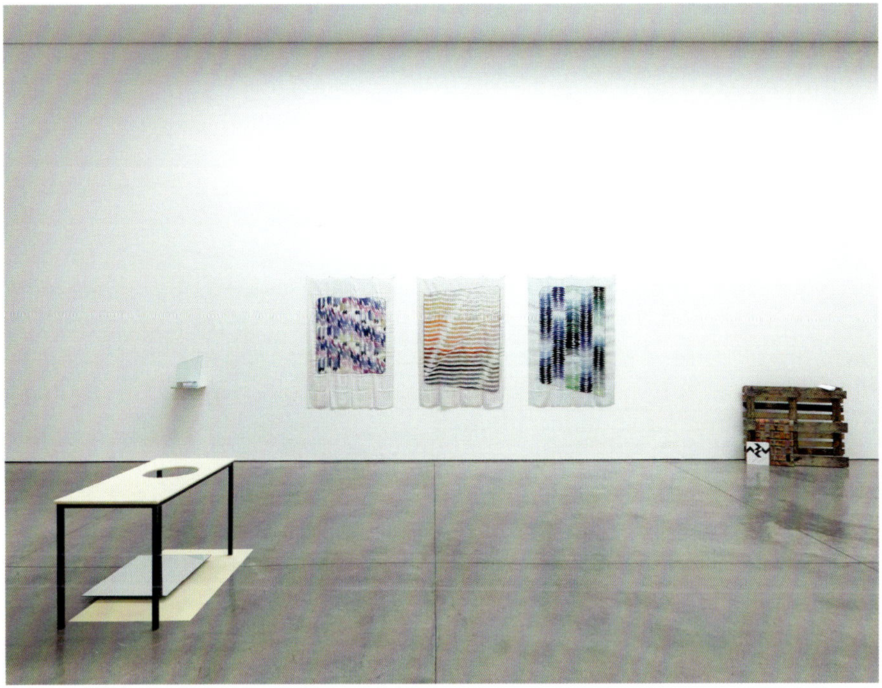

we are prone to becoming close to the artists we work with. The more projects you are involved in and the more artists you know, the more possibilities for favouritism there are. But I cannot stop working with an artist because I have become close to them, and I believe that one needs to draw one's own line in this regard, being true to the work and to the context in your own way, and always being on the lookout for favouritism. The open call is a tool to go beyond one's own immediate community of artists, and in this sense 'Open Cube' was a radical experiment. There are indeed three Brazilians in the show, but that I believe comes from a genuine curiosity and affinity with artists from my own background.

Moving now to the exhibition at White Cube: when we were in Sharjah I was very impressed at how dedicated you were to the selection process. You had about 2,900 applications and you went over each one carefully. What made one artist stand out from another?

To be honest, I wish I could have had more time to go over the applications more carefully. We received about 1,000 online applications on the last day, and to export all of them into a PDF took some time, so in the end there was only about a week for me to see them all, which is when we were in Sharjah. I am quite used to looking at applications and portfolios, but of course I knew I could also rely on the interviews, an essential component of the process. I didn't want to do Skype interviews because I really do believe in live, personal contact; I often travel to a city just to meet an artist. The entire process of looking at so many applications was quite humbling, one that curators should go through from time to time. We did receive applications from all over the world, but I felt it was unreasonable to ask somebody from Asia, Africa or the Americas to come to London for an interview, contacting them less than a week before, so in the end I concentrated on artists based in the UK and in some cases Europe. In this sense the show took on a more local character, although there are artists from different parts of the world.

Initially I wanted to try to put together an exhibition around the notion of the 'white cube' itself – what is inside and outside the gallery, the public and the private space, outdoors and indoors, issues relating to value, currency, commodification and ruins. However, in a process such as this one you need to remain open to the research and allow yourself to respond to the material, in terms of what kind of exhibition can be put together. In this sense, for the interviews, I was selecting artists whose work I thought was somehow intriguing, and at that stage 'intriguing' seemed like a rather vague parameter, but it is a filter that can be used. After the interviews I realised that I could not simply select the most intriguing works, rather I needed to compose groups of works with thematic or conceptual connections. So in the ground-floor gallery, I was able to put together a group closer to the original idea – around the notion of the 'white cube'. On the lower ground-floor gallery, it was geometric abstraction – a Brazilian theme that is familiar to me – which appeared to weave through many of the most interesting works that I saw. Not the traditional, high modernist grid, but certain deviations from and subversions of it, be it through weaving (Caitlin Yardley's *Black Refract (quilt)*; Rodrigo Garcia Dutra's use of Ghanian textiles in *Tabom*; Fay Nicolson's watercolours enlarged and printed on silk in *We Exist! We Have The Will! We Are Producing!)*; natural elements (pollen in Sarah Bernhardt's *Bee Pollen (2/3 Plinth) Pigment (1/3 Plinth)*; goatskin in Caitlin Yardley's *Peripheral Orbit (b)*) and deteriorating media (Nicky Teegan's *Prayer Battery*). There were other very interesting works that I came across during the research, but in order to include them I would have needed a much larger open cube.

You were trained as an artist in Rio de Janeiro, and afterwards did an MFA in Art and Critical Writing at the California Institute of the Arts. In 1998 you were invited by Paulo Herkenhoff to be part of the curatorial team of the 24th São Paulo Biennial, where you were adjunct curator and editor of publications. Since you turned to curating you have always been preoccupied with creating platforms for younger artists to develop, for example when you were curator at the Museu de Arte de Pampulha (2001-03) you created the 'Bolsa Pampulha' for younger artists in Belo Horizonte, then 'PIESP' (Programa Independente da Escola São Paulo) and then 'Laboratório Curatorial' at 'SP-Arte'. Do you think all this emphasis on the development of younger artists and curators comes from the lack of opportunities you had as a young artist?

I believe that one of my strengths lies in developing new programmes in formats that did not exist before, and which respond to the institutional and local contexts – taking advantage of a given infrastructure but also responding to the immediate needs and addressing the deficiencies that I see in that context, so that the programme may have a significant impact.

In Brazil there are few opportunities for younger artists to present and discuss their work in a more in-depth manner, which is why I created the 'Bolsa Pampulha' (Pampulha Grant), at Museu de Arte da Pampulha, in Belo Horizonte, in 2003. At PIESP, at Escola São Paulo, in 2010, I set up an independent study programme for young artists. The biannual year-long programme was my response, as a curator who had trained as an artist, to a certain complacency in the art scene, and the lack of critical discourse among younger artists, particularly at a time of frenzied consumption – the Brazilian market devouring their incipient works, and providing recognition where there was still so much room for development.

'Laboratório Curatorial' is an attempt to find more productive, critical, investigative and educational roles for an art fair, in this case giving the opportunity for a young curator to be engaged in the practice (as opposed to the theory), of putting together an exhibition coupled with the chance to travel, which are two things that are very limited in Brazil. Recently, in this respect, I also spoke to a friend of mine about supporting the creation of grants for young Brazilian curators to participate in ICI's curatorial workshops. The support is small but it can have an impact. I am not even involved in the project, so it is not always about one's own programming. And yes, all these programmes come from my own experience, and my attempt to offer more opportunities to young curators and artists. But I am also interested in offering opportunities to senior artists who have not had recognition, and that is my engagement in 'Spotlight', the project room section at 'Frieze Masters', which I have been able to develop with the support of Victoria Siddall. It is interesting to think that in London two of my projects are being developed in commercial contexts – a gallery and an art fair – and with opposite constituents; the much younger generation of artists and the senior artists, but in both cases I am trying to work with artists who would otherwise not be expected to be exhibiting in these contexts. So in 'Frieze Masters' I am less interested in the traditional, canonical master – the white male European figurative painter – and more concerned with conceptualist or feminist pioneers, such as Nancy Spero, Nil Yalter, Rose English, or artists coming from Africa, Latin America and the Arab world, such as Georges Adéagbo from Benin and Aref Rayess from Lebanon – all of them juxtaposed with more well know figures such a Joseph Kosuth and Gordon Matta-Clark. This all comes from an understanding that as I find myself in a privileged position, with access to certain channels of visibility and production, it is important to take advantage of these opportunities in a more strategic way, bringing artists and curators who would benefit from these projects and whose work I feel could be relevant to our community.

Pablo León de la Barra is an independent curator, researcher and writer, born in Mexico City (1972). He was co-director of '24-7' an artist-curatorial collective in London (2002–05); artistic director of Blow de la Barra, London (2005–08); and founder and co-curator of community art space White Cubicle Gallery, London (2005–12). He has curated numerous exhibitions worldwide, is founder of the Novo Museo Tropical and curated the first Bienal Tropical in San Juan, Puerto Rico (2011). León de la Barra writes extensively for a variety of notable arts publications, has participated in several symposiums and currently serves on the advisory committees of the Cisneros Fontanals Art Foundation, Miami, and the Fundación Luis Barragán, Mexico. In 2013, he was appointed the Guggenheim UBS MAP Curator for Latin America.

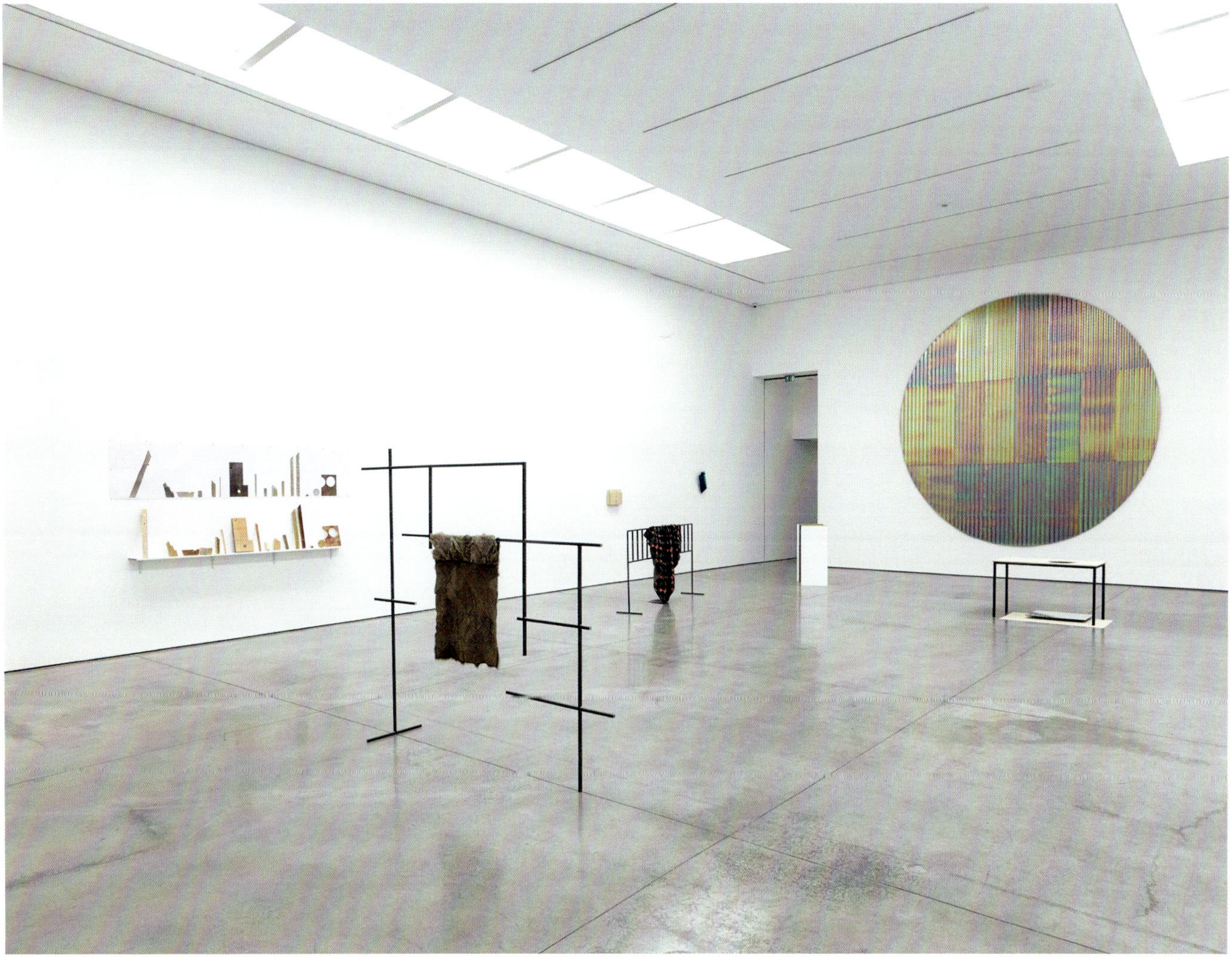

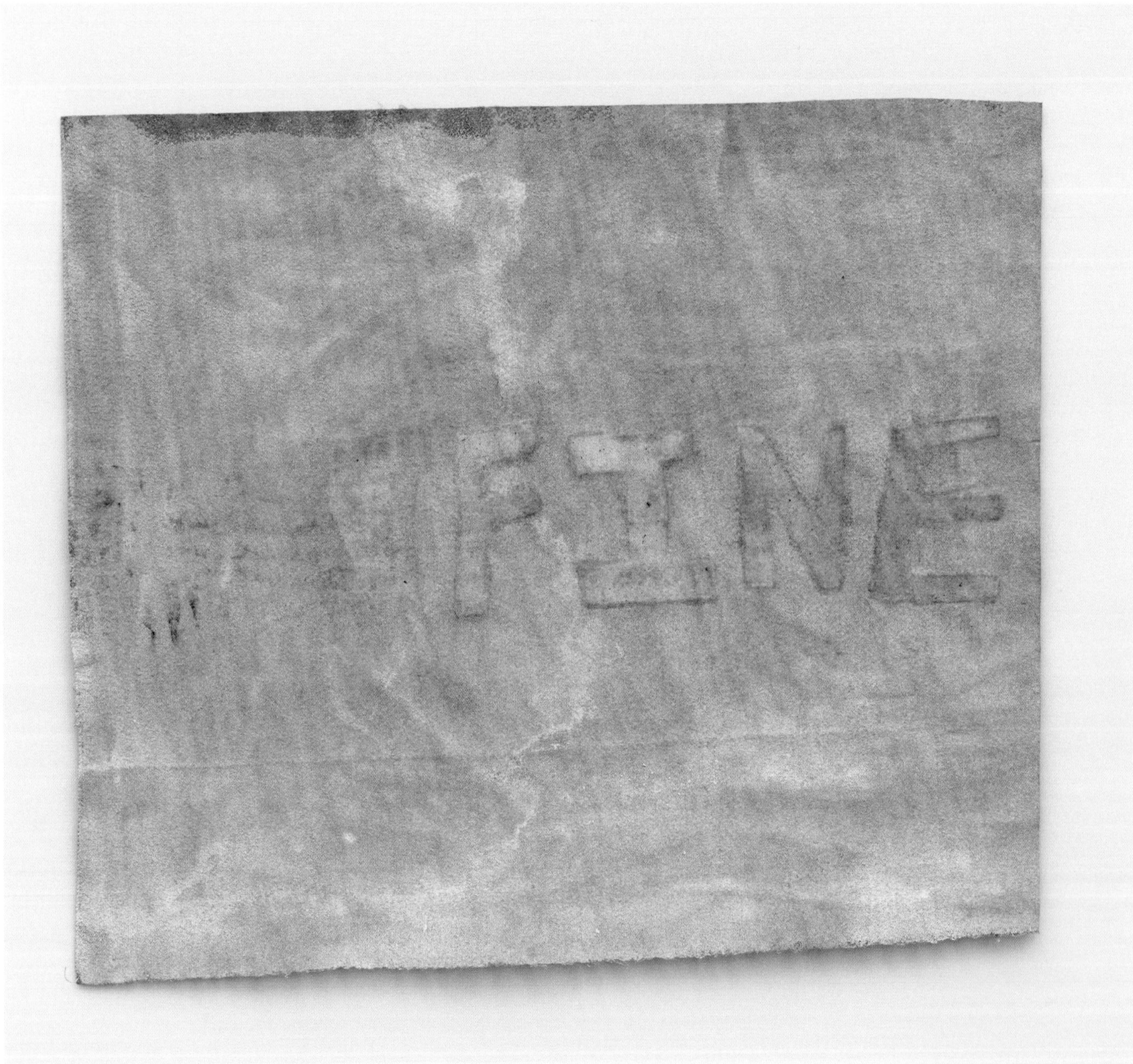
FINE

Matt Ager

Saturday 16 March 2013; 14h30

Adriano Pedrosa: I wanted to ask you why you were interested in participating in 'Open Cube'?
Matt Ager: It's just an exciting premise, to show work in a space that wouldn't normally necessarily facilitate that for younger artists. It's mainly an opportunity to do something that I haven't done before, or something that I felt is an interesting step, to put the work out there in a different context.
How do you perceive White Cube in the context of the London scene?
It's obviously got a huge reputation over the past years in relation to the YBA's, and it's on everybody's radar as something akin to the 'Grande Cube'. It feels like it's currently doing something a little bit more exciting, like with their 'Inside the White Cube' programme and also with its move to Bermondsey. It seems to be somewhere very different from where it was in the past, and it's bringing things that are more current into the local scene. With 'Inside the White Cube' showing younger artists that are doing well and making exciting work alongside artists like Chuck Close, or somebody that is super established. You have two hierarchical systems whereby now it seems more accessible for somebody that is doing something a bit more cool, I think. Having the Eddie Peake show alongside somebody like Chuck Close is kind of an interesting mix.
Have you brought some work?
I did, I brought the piece that you were curious about and I brought a few other bits. There's a discussion I guess I'm trying to have with objects and the position of objects on the wall as well as the relationship between composition of 2- and 3-D, also just experimenting with the

Matt Ager
Fine
2012
Embossed synthetic acrylic
35 7/16 x 35 7/16 in.
(90 x 90 cm)

pictorial plane and how and where that fits in with various different ways of making.

And sometimes photographic as well?

I have made some photographic work.

Like the c-print?

Yes, I did a residency before Christmas in a place in upstate New York where I made these embossings.

May I touch it?

Sure. I used a car to emboss these fairly hard, noncommittal, nonchalant words.

A car?

Yes. I cut them out of MDF and wet the fabric, placed the words underneath the fabric then ran over them with a truck, using it like a press.

With a truck, that's great! And it's called Fine*?*

Yes, it's called *Fine*. I've done several like this. I really like this idea of embossing through sheer pressure.

What is the technique?

This is painted.

So would you say 'mixed media' or 'embossed'?

I think 'embossed'. Embossed text.

I guess you're coming from a painting background?

No, sculpture. I did my BA in Sculpture and am doing my MA in Fine Art.

But are you interested in bringing this into a discussion about the pictorial?

Yes.

As a painting?

As a painting, as a surface that's also been manipulated in some way, shape or form. This was made on the ground and you can see the dirt, you can see the tyre marks, it feels quite dirty and kind of basic. It's a really basic set of materials and a basic process that uses just sheer weight on top of something.

But it does have, if you look at it formally, this complex pictorial surface. Composition, colour, texture.

Yes totally, and I suppose I rely on the gesture as well as the process and the material, as a form of making the work.

Are you interested in it in terms of an accident, or do you have an investment

Matt Ager
Ish
2013
Embossed varnish and acrylic on felt
35 7/16 x 35 7/16 in.
(90 x 90 cm)

in these formal marks?
I have an investment in those marks but it becomes something that is, compositionally perhaps, not at the forefront of the process.
Okay, so it's an accident then in that sense.
It doesn't become a process where I have an idea, draw the idea, then that idea comes to life, but is more about an instinctive making. I made several types because the embossing will only work if the fabric is stiff to a certain extent, so I needed to paint the surface, but in order to paint the surface I needed to choose a colour. There are constant decisions that are made during the making of the work.
One could go back to abstract expressionism and make comparisons with what's going on in the background?
Yes!
It seems rather diluted. Is it acrylic?
Yes, it's white household paint.
What is the fabric?
It's a blanket.
Did it have an original colour?
The reason why it looks like it's faded blue is because it has this whitewash on it. You can still see these parts of the original blanket where it shows through.
And other than that, it's just white paint or is it more?
There are literally coats and coats of white paint.
Always white paint and then the other colours that we see there are just the dirt from running over it with the truck?
Yes, it sort of stained it. It's not just dirt that comes off. I did a few of these, some of which didn't work, so I ended up cutting it down as it was quite big. But it's like 100% polyester cheap blanket. I want it to become something that you can alleviate from its original function.
And the blanket has a history itself, of where it's come from or it's personal...
No, it's from Walmart!
Oh, so you bought it for that, it has not been used.
It's not been used but it was bought intentionally, to paint the surface and emboss on it. But I'm questioning all these different ideas because you've got the idea of the 'found object' and where that comes from and whether it has a use or not, and then seeing the history of those uses is potentially really interesting in the fabrication of a work, or a sculpture

Matt Ager
Perspex fade (glassware)
2012
Painted Perspex and flag holder
15 3/4 x 9 13/16 x 3 1/8 in.
(40 x 25 x 8 cm)

or a surface. But at the same time the idea of 'found' is something that I'm battling with – this idea of where that 'found' can be. Whether you find it in a store and it has a history, someone else's history or whether it has your history.

But do you call this a found object?

Not necessarily.

What, because you bought it, it's a 'bought' object?

I guess I always have the same criteria in my head when making decisions on what I see. Whether I'm walking around outside the store or inside the store, I'm not sure where that difference comes in, in terms of art making: whether the object was outside and somebody else had been using it or whether it was a new-found thing in a different context.

Yes, it's still a deliberate choice. You go there and you find it and buy it with a specific aim in mind.

Yes. For this I was using the blue of this fabric to upholster this piece of wood for another work. So the rest of this blanket existed in another piece of work and then this came as an offcut. I was on a residency, I had no materials with me and I went to the store to buy some materials to make work from. At the time I kind of didn't know what I was going to do with it, but then it became part of the process.

And you said this is not the first one, you have done others?

Yes, I did some before I left for that residency.

So you've done others running over them with the truck?

I did some on an embossing press, which was my first investigation for these works, like for these ones, which are a lot more subtle.

But in terms of the truck, Fine *is the first one?*

Yes, using a truck.

Matt Ager was born in 1985 in England and lives and works in London. He holds a BA in Sculpture from Camberwell College of Arts (2008) and completed a residency at Skowhegan School of Painting and Sculpture, Maine, USA in 2011. He is currently part of the Postgraduate Programme at the Royal Academy Schools, London. Recent exhibitions include 'Classic Poncho', The China Shop, Oxford (2013); 'A Nod', Space In Between, London (2012); 'OVERTHIN', Gallery Primo Alonso, London (2011) and DUMBO Arts Festival, Brooklyn, USA (2010).

Adriano Amaral

Monday 18 March 2013; 10h00

Adriano Pedrosa: Before we start looking at the work I wanted to ask you why you applied to 'Open Cube' and why you were interested in participating in the project and exhibiting here at the gallery.
Adriano Amaral: I guess because it's a really good opportunity to show my work in a nice way in a really good place, and also it's a chance to meet very interesting people from the art community. I really like this idea of using a private gallery in a democratic way; trying to bring in new, fresh artists that do not necessarily engage with the gallery. There are a lot of artists in the world and not much space for everyone, so in a way this is a chance to make things a little bit more fair I think.
What about the gallery itself? You've been in the UK for a year you said?
Yes.
You've been following the programme of the gallery a little bit. Did you know about the gallery before?
Yes. I don't follow every exhibition, but I went to the last exhibition by Kris Martin. I mean everyone knows White Cube. It's one of the most important galleries and personally I really like some artists that are here. But it's a very diverse selection of artists of course. Artists like Anselm Kiefer and Doris Salcedo are two artists that I really like.
They're now working with Jac Leirner, and doing a show with Marcius Galan as well.
Marcius Galan as well?
Yes.
That's really nice, I know him. That's really cool.
Okay, let's talk a little bit about some of the pieces you've presented here. I was quite curious about Untitled (column), *from 2013, which I believe was*

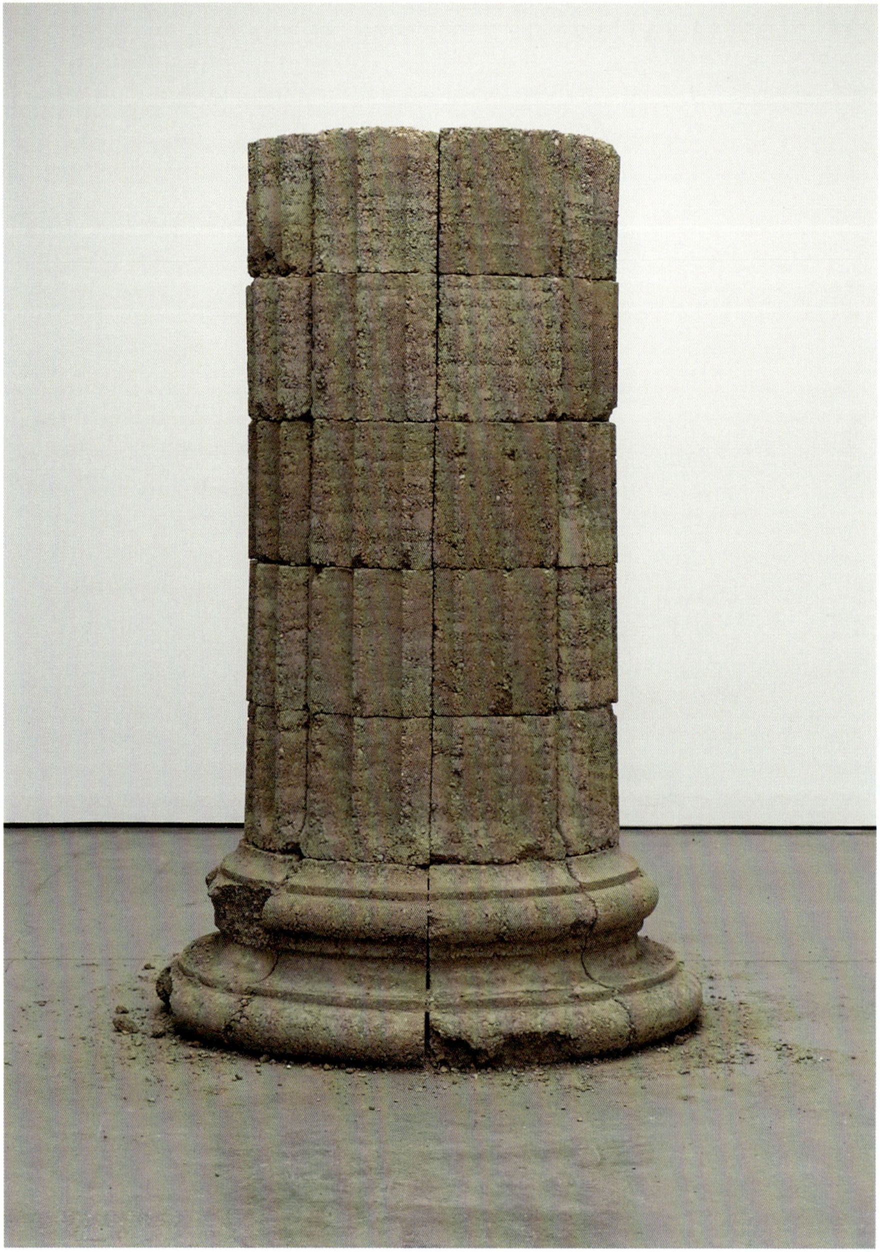

recently presented.
Yes, this is my latest work. This was in the interim show at the Royal College of Art.
Which is like a mid-spring show?
It was in February, so in the winter, but was actually our first show, because the MA course is two years, so basically we have this interim show in the first year and then the final show in the second year. I made this work as site-specific and, well, the work changes a lot during the process.
Is this an image from the first day?
No. There was a photographer from the RCA who took some pictures afterwards so those pictures aren't mine. The work is made from ruins, which is important for me.
Rubble?
Yes. I was thinking about how I could do something with this material because I'm interested in this idea of time, entropy, of the deterioration of things. I started playing with this material which is made from demolished buildings, but they use it to make pavements. They crush it until it becomes almost like sand, very fine. I was thinking about how I could do something that talks about time, about entropy without being nostalgic, and trying to engage with the architecture that surrounds it. So my idea was to place this column as a contrast, this very classical shape, against this modernist building with several very modernist columns.
What kind of column is it that you've made; the design of the column?
I think its Doric but I always get confused!
I do too.
Between Ionic and Doric. I know that it's not Corinthian. Corinthian is the one that has...
Right, but you didn't use it?
No, I just used the base of the column.
Did it get destroyed later or was it like this from the beginning?
No, the initial idea wasn't to have it collapse, but it collapsed on the way to the RCA gallery.
Oh right, so this is not made on site, it's made elsewhere and then you transported it.
Yes.
But it's super delicate, no?
Yes.

Adriano Amaral
Untitled (column)
2013
Reclaimed construction materials
Dimensions variable

How tall is it?
I think two and a half metres.
Were you looking at specific columns somewhere?
Yes, this became important in the end but I didn't think about it too much when I was doing it. I took measurements from a column in the British Museum. There is this round skylight in the RCA gallery, so when I say it's site-specific it's because my first idea was to place this column as if it passed through this skylight. I just found this would be the right place to put it. Almost like, stuck in the building.
As if it was actually supporting something?
Yes, and not really supporting, because it's so huge and so awkward, like it doesn't really seem like it's supporting something, but as if it's two different times stuck together, our time now and this different period of time that, suddenly, is still there. I was thinking about, more or less, a contrast, and I really like the idea of putting it in the way, so it obstructs you – uncomfortable in a way. So a lot of things changed because as you can see it's divided into several pieces, almost like breeze blocks. For each ring there are eight pieces.
Okay, so they are transported like that?
Yes.
And do you put anything in the rubble, in order for it to become compacted or something?
I use water because I made a mould.
Just water?
Water and a little bit of PVA glue. I mix it a little bit. But I really wanted to have this crumbling look.
So you were happy with the results or would you do something different with it?
Yes. I really like it.
I mean the fact that it was, you know, destroyed and then you thought it was okay, it's fine and you're happy with that?
Yes I think...
Because it was an accident and then you just incorporated that?
Exactly, totally.

Adriano Amaral was born in 1982 in Brazil and lives and works in London. He is currently studying for an MA in Sculpture at the Royal College of Art, London. Recent exhibitions include 'WIP Show', Royal College of Art, London (2013); 'Embaixo da Terra o Céu de Novo', Galeria Transversal, São Paulo (2012); 'Solo Objects', Arco Madrid (2012) and 'Nova Escultura Brasileira', Caixa Cultural, Rio de Janeiro (2011).

Frank Ammerlaan

Sunday 17 March 2013; 17h00

Adriano Pedrosa: I wanted to ask you, before we start to look at the work, why you are interested in participating in 'Open Cube'?
Frank Ammerlaan: I've done a couple of commercial projects recently, in terms of the commercial gallery, and have just come back from New York, where I had a presentation at 'The Armory Show'. It was interesting to do, but I'm actually looking now for an exhibition or project, where I can have a conversation about the possibilities of doing something in situ.
I see. Site-specific?
Yes, which I think is not the primary focus of my practice, but when I work towards an exhibition and I finally know what the space is, I try to make work that relates to the space. I do make work in the studio, which you could almost see as chapters, and then the total exhibition or combination of these is maybe the script. In the end I like to combine the works that I have already made with works specifically related to the space, to the concept.
Okay, so let's look at the images you've sent.
This is a work that came out of a film I saw called *Day's End* by Gordon Matta-Clark.
Yes, I was reading that reference in the PDF you sent.
For me it was just about the first few seconds of the film. It is a 20 minute film in which Matta-Clark starts cutting out a circle in the wall, which slowly lets the light into this abandoned warehouse on a pier on the Hudson River. I thought it was a very positive sign actually; a relationship between the abandonedness and the sadness of the surroundings. This work is made from corrugated steel, which is the same material as the side of the warehouse in the film.

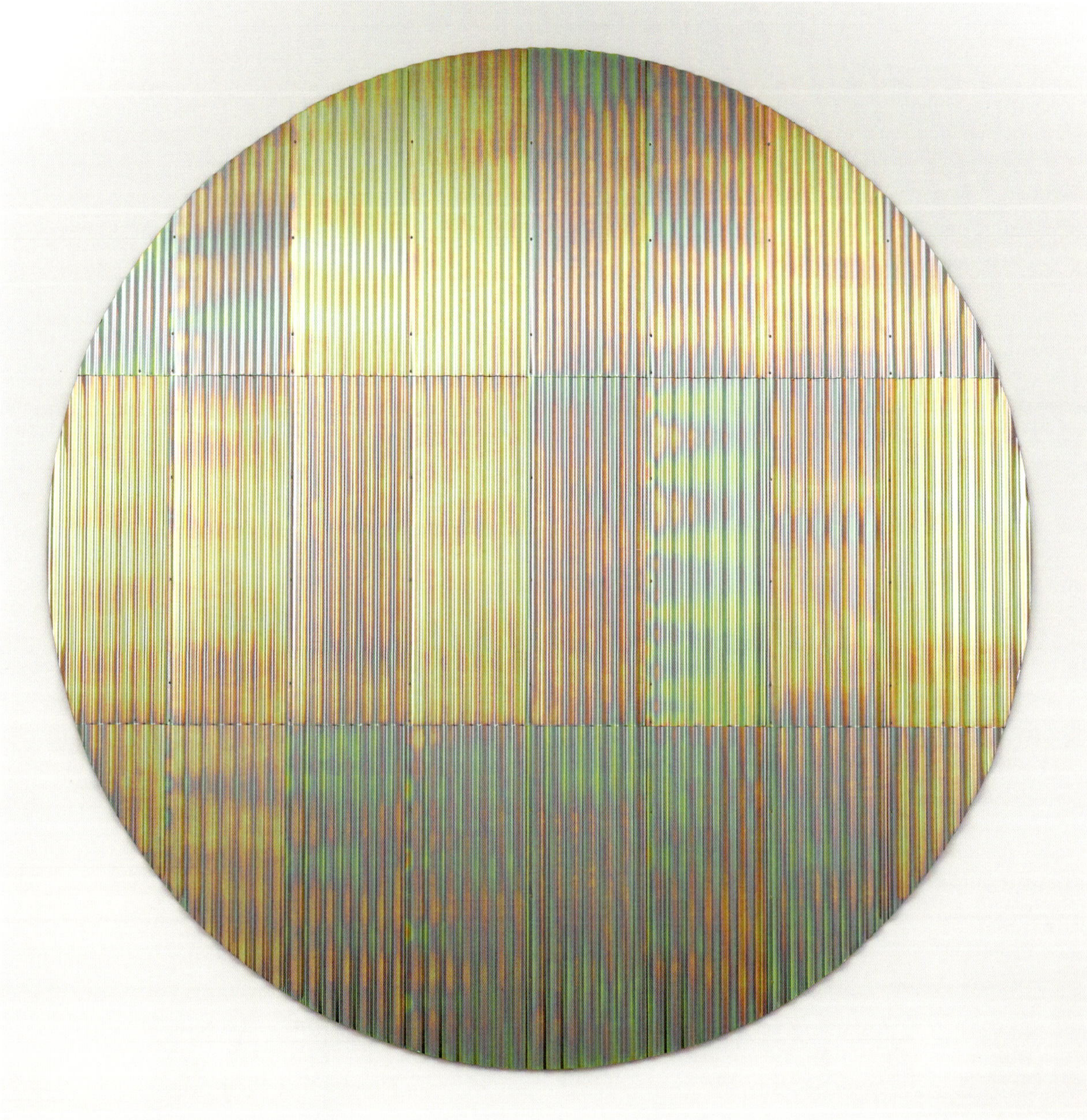

Yes, but when I read that it did strike me that of course Matta-Clark's gesture is quite experimental, there's not an object there, while your work is very much an object?
It's almost like the residue, but in that sense it doesn't relate too much to the work of Matta-Clark. To me it was just the first gesture.
Anyhow, it's just the text that you provided. It's not even in the title, it's just your own justification, no?
Exactly. I took the title *Day's End* from his work.
Yes, but the title is open enough for you to deviate from it.
Very much so.
To be honest with you, if I saw that, I would probably think of a sunset, and this is a presentation of a landscape somehow and it's reflective, in the photograph it's probably reflecting the light.
What you see is an assembly of ten different sheets of electroplated corrugated steel. Each sheet has been dipped into twenty different electrically charged chemical baths to achieve their finish.
Oh I see! So you got to this effect by chemical manipulation?
It's called 'colour passivated zinc'. It's a finish that goes onto metal to prevent it from rusting. It's the cheapest way to prevent it from rusting, but you only find it on small parts like screws, or probably in your phone.
I see. Okay they don't do it in large pots like that?
They don't. I found a company in Birmingham that does, and I like this idea that probably these paintings or works are hung on screws that have this finish. And, these objects always operate in your peripheral vision. Just outside your focus. So this work is about 2 metres 70 cms I think, but the walls are very nice and long. I mean it wouldn't work if the wall was as wide as long, I think it needs a bit of wall.
Yes, some breathing space. You put it together because it's quite large to transport? Is this on the ground floor?
It's in ten different parts. It's like when you make a building, they put it on top of each other.
Right, but you don't screw it or you don't fix it?
It's screwed.
But you can assemble it and disassemble it as you need, to transport and install it?
Exactly, and there is also a bit of space between the work and the wall. It gives it a little bit of shadow on the wall.
But are you also interested in the sunset, the landscape reference and the pictorial

Frank Ammerlaan
Day's End
2013
Colour passivated zinc on steel
Ø 172 7/16 in. (Ø 438 cm)

and how that plays?
Well I wouldn't necessarily say the sunset, but it's this idea of changeability; the changeability that comes, for example, with dusk and dawn, when you see literally, or almost feel literally, that the Earth is moving.
You have daylight, this is daylight, so the piece does change quite a lot during the day and the night?
A lot of works do actually.
A lot of your work you mean?
Yes. I have works where I embroider fluorescent and metallic threads into the work. When you move around the painting the light starts running on the thread and… It's better on the other image. This one is a little bit more subtle, it's harder to see on the other image. There are different kinds of thread embroidered in the painted surface.
I see, mostly squares, rectangles. What about the chemical paintings?
With the chemical ones I like to start from the idea. It started with a very mundane phenomenon; it's a perfect day today, when it rains and you see the spills from the motorised vehicles on the streets in the form of oil spills; it's a very elusive thing, if the water evaporates it's gone, it's non-material. So I went to a chemist and said, 'Oh okay, how can we make this physical, materialise it, so it stays?' I like to start from that kind of angle. Not only to work with materials and have an interesting kind of aesthetic or result. Finally, it took about one and a half years to work with the chemist and in the end it became a process where the painting lies in a bath, I fill it up with water until there's a little layer of water above the surface of the canvas. Then I pour a transparent mixture of chemicals into the water, and when it hits the water it kind of 'phew', explodes. Then I drain the water out and slowly the film that floats on the water, settles on the canvas.
And how long does it take, the whole process?
Not long.
And to dry?
Just like, two hours.
So this takes one day to do?
Yes, it's very fast.
And do you add any pigment?
No.

Frank Ammerlaan
Untitled
2013
Chemicals on canvas
68 7/8 x 61 in.
(175 x 155 cm)

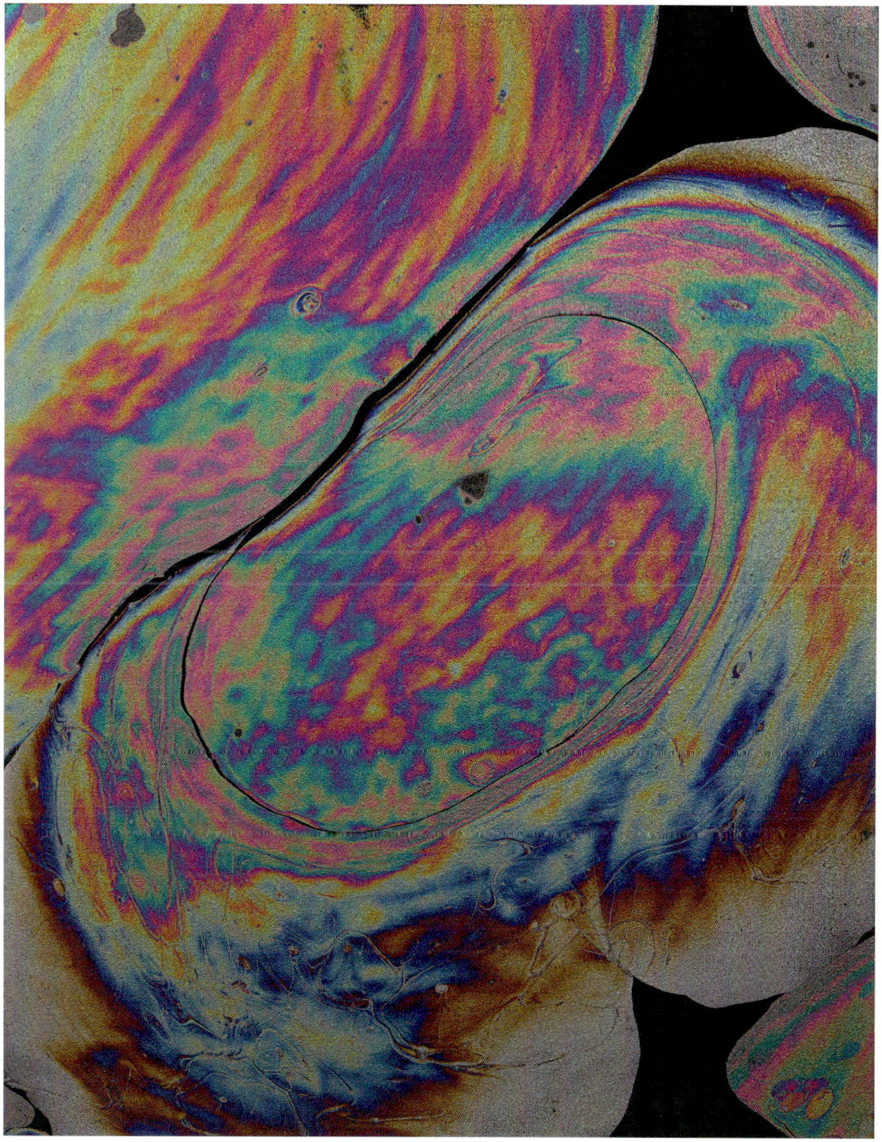

It's just...
Pure chemical.
You can change the amount or the composition of the amount or percentages?
No.
How many chemicals?
The thing is, because it's a component of chemical materials and it's all chemical names, I don't know really what they are.
Okay, but you have that mixture and it's always the same mixture?
Yes, yes.
And the same amount maybe?
Yes.
How many have you made so far?
I think maybe fifteen.
And you started last year in 2012?
The first one I showed at the Royal College of Art, in my degree show. There was one of 3 by 2 metres.
3 by 2 metres! You need a pretty big sort of...
Yes it was big. I had to build a huge bath and also in that case I knew which space I had for my degree show, which was a space with very high ceilings, so I made a work that related to the, how do you say it?
The scale?
The scale of the space.
Of the space?
Yes.
And it's interesting also when you have some sort of natural change in light, no?
I mean they're unbelievably intense in terms of colour, they're holographic. If you move around, they start vibrating and moving.
Which is something you also found in the metallic piece.
Exactly.

Frank Ammerlaan was born in 1979 in Sassenheim, The Netherlands and lives and works in London. He holds a BA in Fine Art from the Gerrit Rietveld Academie, Amsterdam (2007) and an MA in Painting from the Royal College of Art, London (2012). Ammerlaan has participated in residencies at the Museum of Contemporary Art, Calasetta, Italy (2013); Royal Award of Painting, The Netherlands (2012) and Land Securities Studio Award, 'Degree Show', Royal College of Art, London (2012). Recent exhibitions include a solo presentation at 'The Armory Show', New York (2013); 'Painting without Paint', David Risley Gallery, Copenhagen (2012); 'Day's End', Upstream Gallery, Amsterdam and 'Stereopsis', Drawing Room, London (2012).

Helen Barff

Monday 18 March 2013; 17h00

Adriano Pedrosa: I wanted to ask you why you applied and why you were interested in participating in this exhibition?
Helen Barff: Well it seemed like a great opportunity really. I was curious to see what you would do with an open submission, because I thought it would be interesting to see what an open show would be like when it's strongly curated in some respect, as they can be a jumble sale of work.
And what about the gallery itself? Do you follow a little bit of the gallery's programme?
I do. I haven't come here for a while, but I've been here a lot, and I'm familiar with it. And the Bermondsey space too.
And how do you perceive the gallery itself?
One of the more interesting ones I'd say. Well, it's one of the main galleries showing the main people. I was surprised they were doing an open submission.
I proposed it to them.
Oh did you?
They asked me to do a group exhibition and I proposed an open call.
I was surprised, I didn't think...
It's an experiment. It's never really been done I think with a gallery such as this one, a very high-end, blue-chip, prestigious gallery. I'm also doing this because I'm interested in opening up the process, and that in fact is why we are recording the interviews.
I mean, it's interesting because this gallery shows people like Anselm Kiefer and people like that. Like, really huge artists of this century and the last century. I teach and it's somewhere I send students to look, because it's more like a museum at times.

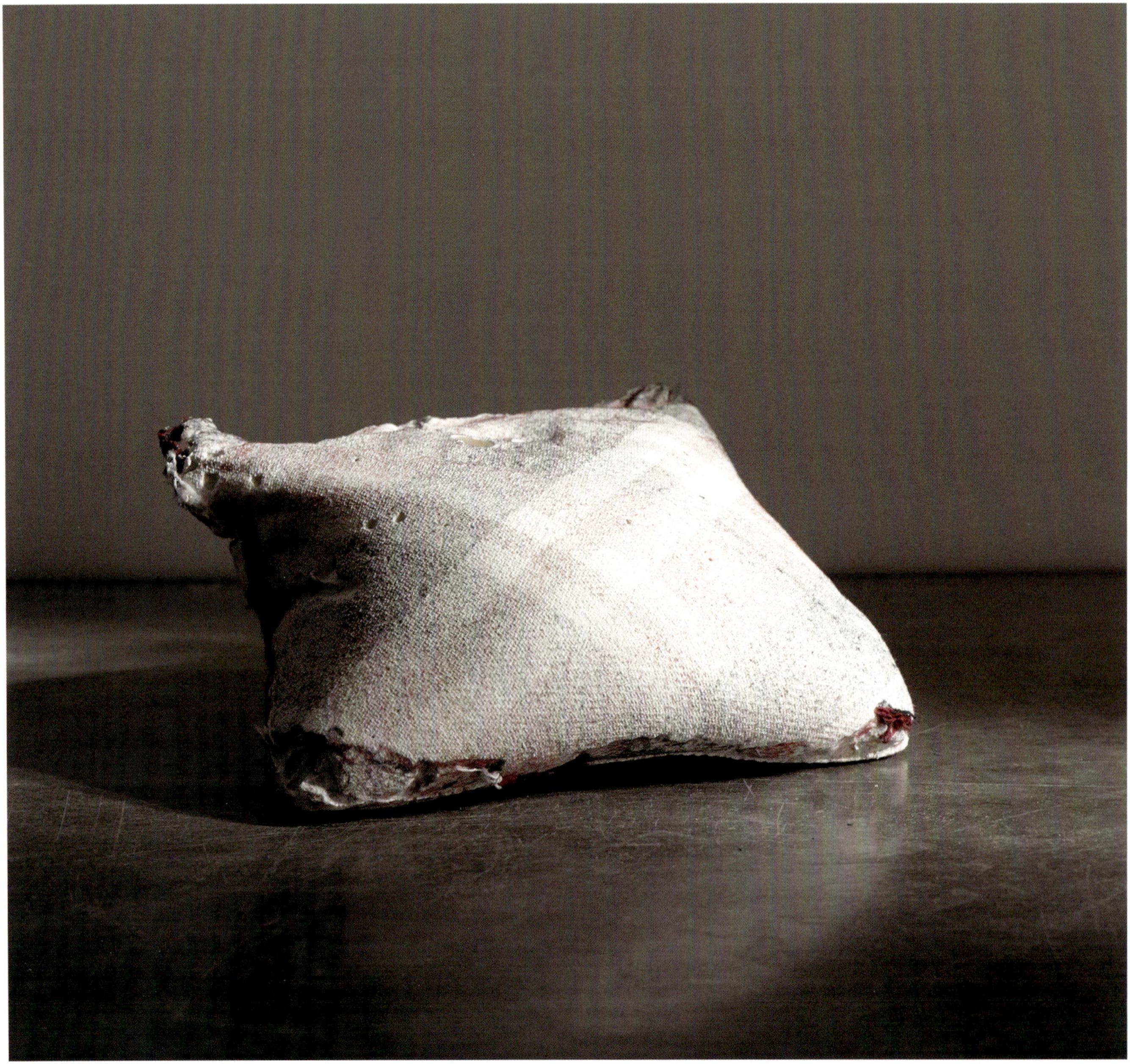

So tell me about Pockets *then, from 2011.*
The pockets developed out of a series of work where I cast the inside of clothes. I took clothes apart and stitched them together again in different formations, filled them with plaster and then took off the fabric. You can see that it leaves a sort of trace of threads, and bits and pieces, and the idea with this and a lot of my work is that the sense of touch is very central. I was looking at the skin I guess, and the points of contact you have inside your clothes, those sort of hidden spaces. It relates back to previous work to do with the surface of things.
Does the colour come from the clothing?
Yes, mainly. Some of them I added a bit of colour, but most of it comes from the clothing. These are concrete, the darker ones.
The plaster is rather fragile, no?
Yes, it's quite fragile.
The concrete is more solid?
Yes, although concrete, when it's cast in very thin bits is fragile.
Is that a single piece we are looking at or is it 9 different pieces?
There are about 25 of those altogether.
Are they all individual or is it a single piece?
I think it would depend where they were installed.
Well it depends really how they're sold.
Yes.
Sold or circulated.
I don't see them as a finite number.
So you wouldn't exhibit a single one for example?
I have exhibited a single one.
Okay. So it's looser at this point because you haven't really finalised them for circulation?
Exactly!
Let's say, beyond them being your own property, no?
Yes, exactly.
These are different pieces of clothing that you've sewn together?
Yes, either my own clothing or clothing that I have collected from other people, then reconfigured and filled with plaster. There are others that sit on the floor; there are all different kinds. They became these sort of anthropomorphic creatures that are quite comic and

Helen Barff
Pocket 11
2011
Plaster
2 3/8 x 4 3/4 x 4 5/16 in.
(6 x 12 x 11 cm)

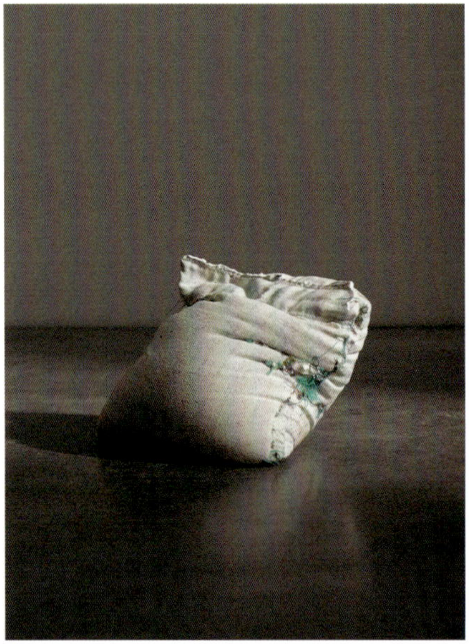
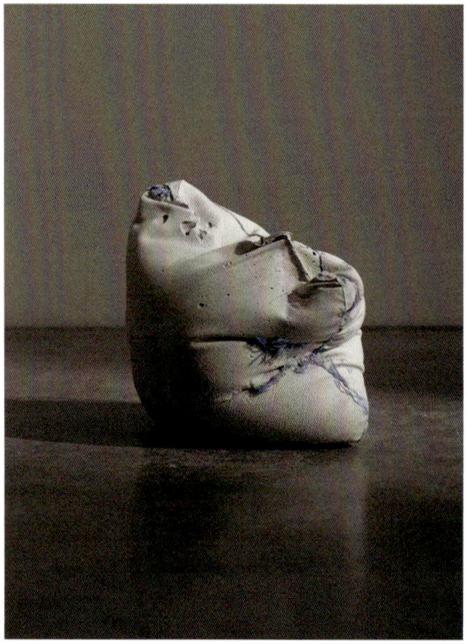
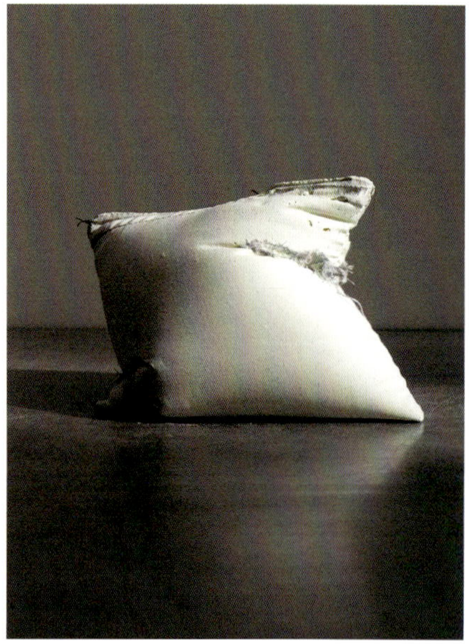
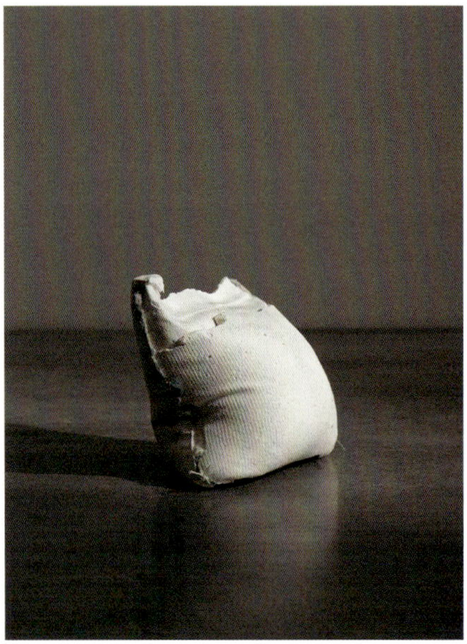
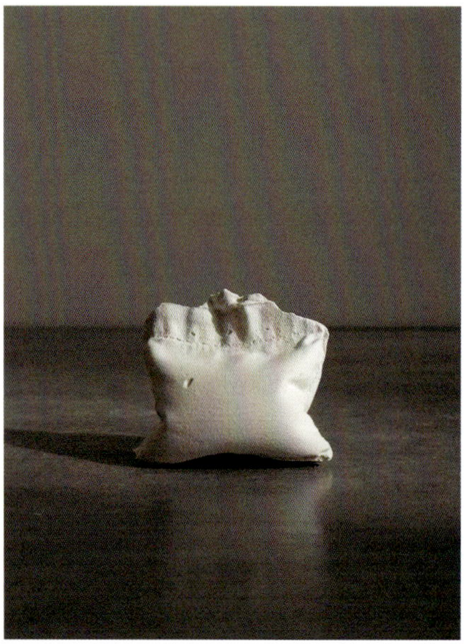
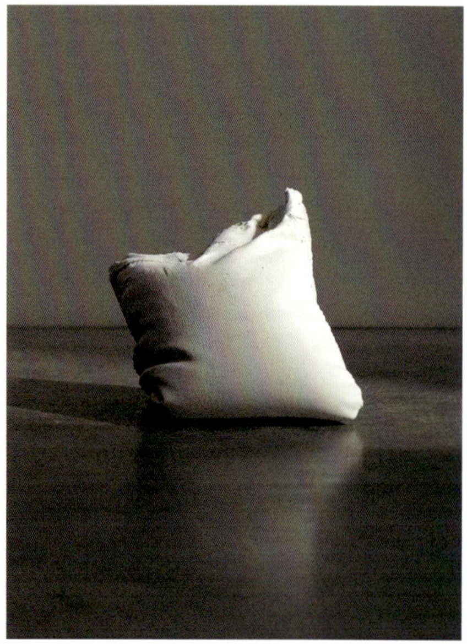

sexual in a way, these strange beings that came about. The title, *Brood*, seemed to fit with them. You can see with my 'bump' the sort of stage of life I'm at.

Congratulations!

I was producing these strange creatures at the same time as I was producing my own.

So these are very recent?

No, those were from 2011, but I'm still doing them, so I've developed them further. I've also made ones that sit on the floor and grow out of the walls.

So this is concrete?

That's concrete.

The texture is fantastic.

I wish I'd brought the work along for you to see. It's lovely. It's furry.

It really looks like a fabric piece.

Yes, they do.

But these are not pockets are they, this one that I'm looking at?

That's the inside of a pocket.

They look like the pockets themselves. Okay, so this one is concrete, and this one?

That's plaster; the lighter ones are plaster.

And did you put colour on these, so that it is greenish?

That's from the fabric. It's just picked up from the fabric.

It looks like jeans or something? Is it green jeans?

No, it's a shirt, but a shirt that has a slightly textured fabric, one of those check shirts. But it does look like fabric, and when people look at them they think they are fabric, but the fabric has been removed. They look like sacks, little fabric sacks. I did some different sizes and jean pockets as well. The idea partly came out of the clothing and the idea of this inside space, the space where your hands are, a secret space I guess. Also, I always liked that Samuel Beckett poem about stones, where he moves stones from one pocket to another.

And these pockets were all arranged on the shelf?

Yes.

So these really have a different quality to them?

Yes, they're a different series of work really.

How long is the shelf roughly?

That shelf didn't have all of them on actually, I had them kind of stacked.

top left to bottom right:
Helen Barff
Pocket 4, 6, 12, 15, 16, 22
2011
Plaster or concrete
Dimensions variable

But ideally you imagine them on a shelf, one next to each other? Say there were 27. This is 10, probably 27 cm. 27, that's 2, equals 540.

Yes.

5 metres.

Some of them are smaller; some are from smaller pockets, so they vary.

So, with the round ones, 4 metres maybe?

They tend to be on different shelves. But if you had a really long shelf… It would be nice on a long shelf, to show the continuality of them.

And did you choose the grey colour of the shelf?

Yes.

You wanted the grey against the white wall, no?

I like the kind of neutrality of grey. I think white can be a very harsh colour behind the works. This photograph was actually just set up in my studio, so that wasn't in the exhibition space.

Do you have any photographs of the pockets in the exhibition space?

No. The pockets have only been exhibited once and I wasn't totally happy with the way they were presented. It was in an old church, so what you could do was restricted; you couldn't drill into the walls and things, and we had them all randomly presented.

Oh right, a table or something?

Yes, and it didn't quite work for me.

I think at this stage it would be useful if you could send me more images. I mean, if you have images of all of them, even if it's just your snapshots.

I don't have images of all of them but I could set it up easily in my studio, and just take some snaps of them all and send them to you, if that's okay?

That will be great because it would be nice to see them in more detail.

I think with these, because it's sort of an ongoing thing, it's not like there *has* to be 27 pockets. There are 27 at the moment, but there could be more, or less, it's just an ongoing…

Are you interested in investigating the sculptural, as they are very sculptural?

They're very sculptural, yes.

Sort of traditional formal issues of sculpture: inside and outside, the weight, the material.

Yes, I totally agree.

Negative-positive.

Exactly. As well as the sense of touch that I see as part of that, and our own bodies. The inside and outside of us is a continual space. The topology of skin. I'm also fascinated by the ways that objects 'sit', and the space between them. I guess that's quite old-fashioned or traditional in a way.

And also the intimate scale.

Yes, people always want to touch them. When they were exhibited previously people were told not to touch them, but I knew they did because they moved.

They are fascinating. They don't look like the material that they are.

No, they don't.

This one for instance looks like something else. These in the low resolution image that I'm looking at, appear as though they've been stitched, and they've aged.

They do, and all the pockets are used pockets.

Of course, and it's interesting that this registers and is evident in the cast.

Yes.

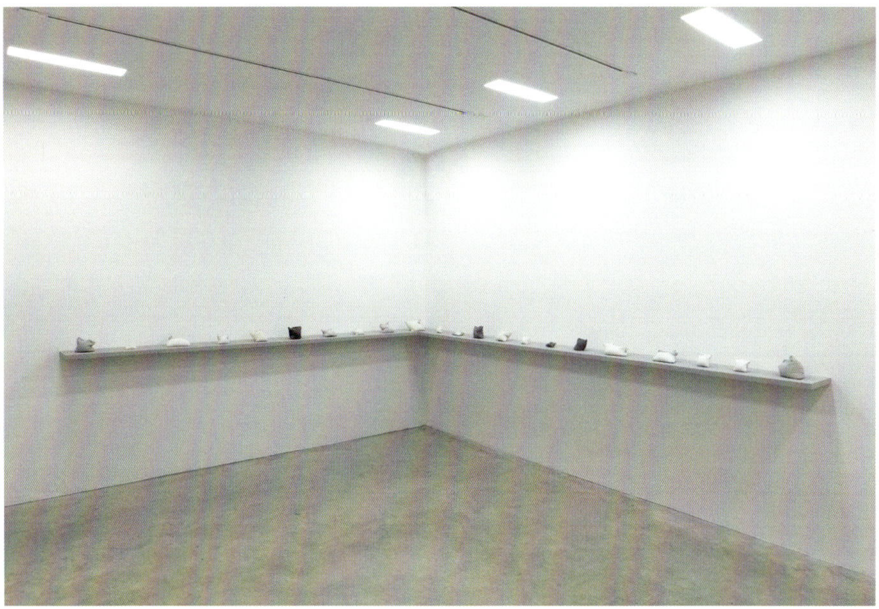

Helen Barff
Pocket 1–22
2011
Plaster or concrete
Dimensions variable

Whereas you would think the cast would clean-up, or erase the history of the materials, but it actually imprints them, does that make sense?
Yes, it does.
I feel, as I'm looking at them in these digital images, that they're cuddly as well.
They are, they are little creatures. I mean, all the ones in the plaster, and the other clothing ones too became like these little soft toys or something. They look like they should be soft, and people touch them and expect them to be soft.
They wouldn't be as interesting if they were soft, which is something I think you know because that's how it plays off. This really looks like it's a realist painting, but it's not really what it looks like.
Yes.
It seems like a soft thing. There's a Brazilian artist, Ernesto Neto, I wonder if you've heard of him?
No.
He had a big show at The Hayward Gallery a couple of years ago.
Oh yes. I didn't recognise the name at first because you pronounced it correctly!
There's some connection it seems.
In fact I was kind of influenced a bit by him in some of the new stuff I made. You saw that I did some things with boat shapes that I haven't resolved yet. A fabric boat that's suspended, that was partly influenced by him.

Helen Barff was born in 1974 in England and lives and works in London. She holds a BA in Fine Art and Art History from Goldsmiths College, London (1999) and an MA in Drawing from Camberwell College of Arts, London (2004). She has participated in a residency at Greatmore Studios, Cape Town (2008), through the Triangle Arts Trust and Gasworks, London. Recent exhibitions include 'Brood', Bend in the River, Gainsborough, UK (2011); 'Trident Way 2: The Southall Project', Departure Gallery, London (2009); 'Raising Ground', Bearspace, London (2008) and a site-specific project 'Route 12:36', Routemaster, South London Gallery (2000).

Sarah Bernhardt

Monday 18 March 2013; 12h00

Adriano Pedrosa: One question I always ask is why you applied to 'Open Cube' and why you were interested in participating in the exhibition?
Sarah Bernhardt: For me it's that I've never had anyone curate my work before, and when it comes to showing my work I'm almost overly strict about how it's shown, how it's positioned and how it reacts in a space, and I really like having or making art that's removed from the viewer. So, it would be incredible for me to see my work taken over by someone else, or have someone else look at it from a totally different angle. I would like to step back a little.
Is this your most recent work?
Yes. The plinths are the most recent, and the title of this work is *Bee Pollen (2/3 Plinth) Pigment (1/3 Plinth)*.
Was this exhibited somewhere?
It was exhibited at Transition Gallery.
It's a space here?
It's a space in London often showing young artists who are finding their feet, and they're okay with giving people their first shows. They didn't ask me for a CV before I exhibited or anything like that. I think of all the works I've made this is one of the pieces that I'm most satisfied with.
Do you think asking for a CV means that we're looking for something?
Oh for sure.
Like what, if the person has exhibited more or less?
Yes I think so.
More or less?
More, but not for this show as I know that this show is different. 'Open Cube' is different, it's the Sol LeWitt of Cubes, you know.

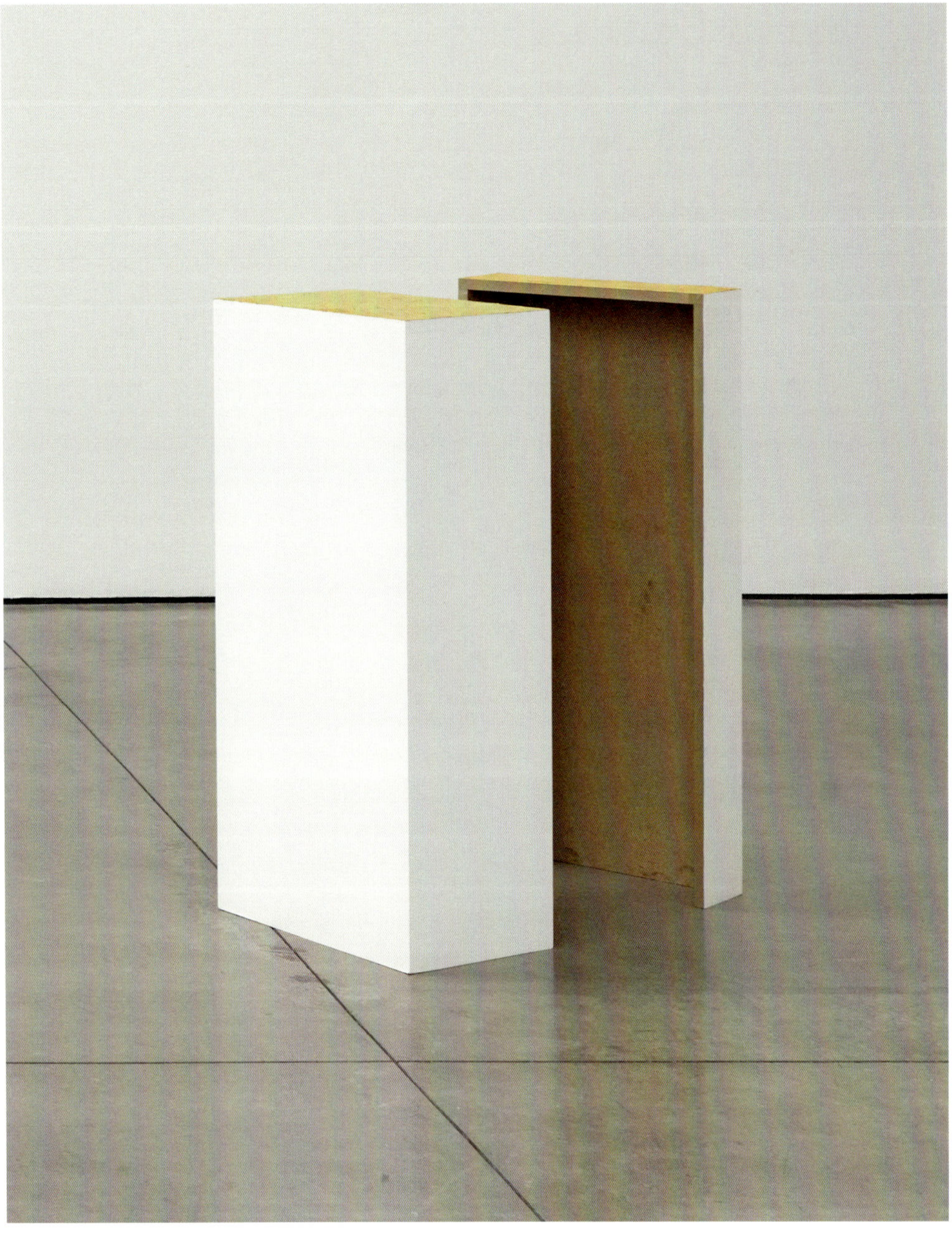

It's open to everyone.
That's very curious, because often when I'm doing research for an exhibition and particularly for a large-scale international show like a biennial, I look at the artist's resume and the fewer things they have done, the more interesting it becomes. It's very singular because you're showing something, and bringing something to the surface that has not really been exhibited before. And I guess for my colleagues too, if an artist has already shown at two or three biennials, it becomes less interesting for us.
Why ask for it then?
Precisely to know if the artist has already been all around the world. It's like, 'He's been to all the biennials already', so consequentially I'm going to show another artist. This is something that people complain about a lot – that 'Oh you always see the same artists'.
Oh I agree.
So we try not to, well at least that's how it is on the projects that I work on. Maybe there are others who do the opposite, looking for artists that have been in all the biennials. I'm sure there are those curators.
I think that's really amazing. I've only had one show with this work.
Can you tell me why you think this work is one of the more successful works that you've done?
I think I'm most interested in what I'm working on now or the things that happened most recently. This is the last piece of work I made and I'd like to move on from it. I think often I'm interested in coming back to iconic modes of presentation or slightly maligned modes of presentation.
Slightly?
I wanted to use a plinth for a long time and I also wanted to work with bee pollen. I've done a lot of work using natural pigments, raw pigments, but have never used bee pollen. For a while I thought, okay, never work with bee pollen because of Wolfgang Laib. I worry that you can't really use another artist's materials and I was anxious about that.
When did you discover that Wolfgang Laib had used pollen?
I've known that for a while, and I was thinking about how I would use pollen without quoting someone else? The artist that I kept coming back to when making this piece wasn't Wolfgang Laib, but Felix Gonzalez-Torres. I think his *Untitled (Perfect Lovers)* is my favourite piece of art. You have two mechanical, almost kitchen-like wall clocks hung slightly off-

Sarah Bernhardt
Bee Pollen (2/3 Plinth)
Pigment (1/3 Plinth)
2013
Paint, MDF, bee pollen and pigment
39 3/8 x 17 11/16 x 12 3/16 in. (100 x 45 x 31 cm) and
39 3/8 x 17 11/16 x 5 1/2 in. (100 x 45 x 14 cm)

centre set to the same time, but as the work progresses it opens up a negative space and provides the ability to be able to look into that space. It's just such a beautiful, melancholic statement to make about things that are 'one', or are so similar that you can't differentiate whether they were ever separated or not.

Can you tell me more about the material in your work?

The top of the two-thirds plinth is covered in bee pollen, which has quite a pungent smell when you're close to the installation. The top of the one-third plinth is covered with a pigment that is colour matched – a mechanical pigment – to be like the bee pollen. It's very important that the placement of these are exactly right, so that as you move around the plinths the gaps between them become more and less apparent – this was what I was really keen on. If you look on the two-thirds plinth you can see burn marks from a circular saw which I thought about getting rid of but I decided to leave them in because I like the raw edges of things; I like to give an idea of how something has been made.

Yes, nice piece.

Up close the surfaces are quite different because the one with bee pollen is obviously thick and undulating, whereas the one with the mechanically matched pigment, or the pigment that I matched myself, is much, much smoother. They don't have the same movement.

And the fact that they are on a plinth, divided into two-thirds and a third? Are you happy with the hollow plinth?

Yes, yes, absolutely.

And the finish inside?

Everything about it.

And that it is painted white.

Yes of course.

Is it perfectly painted? Is it a different type of white paint?

It's the usual emulsion you would use to paint a plinth that would support a sculpture in an exhibition. It's very standard, and I really like the way the MDF looks.

Oh, it's MDF?

Yes. It's such an ugly material but it's also so beautiful, and I quite like to fetishize it.

What height is it?

I think it's about a metre.
And it forms a square?
It forms an exact square and looks like the sort of plinth that you might associate with video works.
So it's about maybe 40 by 40 cm?
It's slightly bigger – it's 45 by 45 cm. When I was attaching the pigment I used a casein binder which is very natural.
You mentioned Felix Gonzalez-Torres and Untitled (Perfect Lovers), *so do you think this is a romantic reference in terms of the doubling of one third – to equal two thirds – and the idea of something being matched or unmatched?*
I'm not sure I would use the word romantic but I would use the word 'intimate'.
But not in an emotional, psychological way, but more in terms of the materials?
I think it's not as direct. It's very difficult to look at Felix Gonzalez-Torres without knowing about his life and knowing why that piece was made, and when it was made.
But even if you don't know it's called Untitled (Perfect Lovers), *you still have two symmetrical clocks...*
Yes, and it's probably more readily a pair than these, so I feel this is probably more watered down.
Well it's just that Untitled (Perfect Lovers) *is also about this perfect pair which at times mismatch as the timing is off, whereas this is more obviously a mismatch because of it being one-third and two-thirds, yet the colourisation is the same and the material is apparently the same, but it's not even symmetrical and it's also not psychological, it's not bodily, there's not really...*
There's no domestic link either I suppose.
There's not a character here, in terms of a character in a novel. A personality.
There's less narrative I guess.
Whereas with Untitled (Perfect Lovers), *you think about a double portrait, no?*
You think about a diptych.
And a double portrait, if they're perfect lovers.
Yes you would associate...
Each clock represents a lover.
You project a human presence onto it.
But with your work there is no human presence.
There isn't a human presence, but if you stay with it a little bit longer

and look at the fact that it's bee pollen, then I still think there's a gesture behind it, there's something that is natural.
Definitely natural.
Slightly mismatched.
But not human at all, no?
No

Sarah Bernhardt was born in 1989 in Canterbury, UK and lives and works in London. She holds a BA in Fine Art from Central Saint Martin's College of Art and Design, London (2012). Recent exhibitions include 'Co-Respondent', Transition Gallery, London (2013) and 'The Sand Between God's Toes', Pie Factory, Margate, UK (2012).

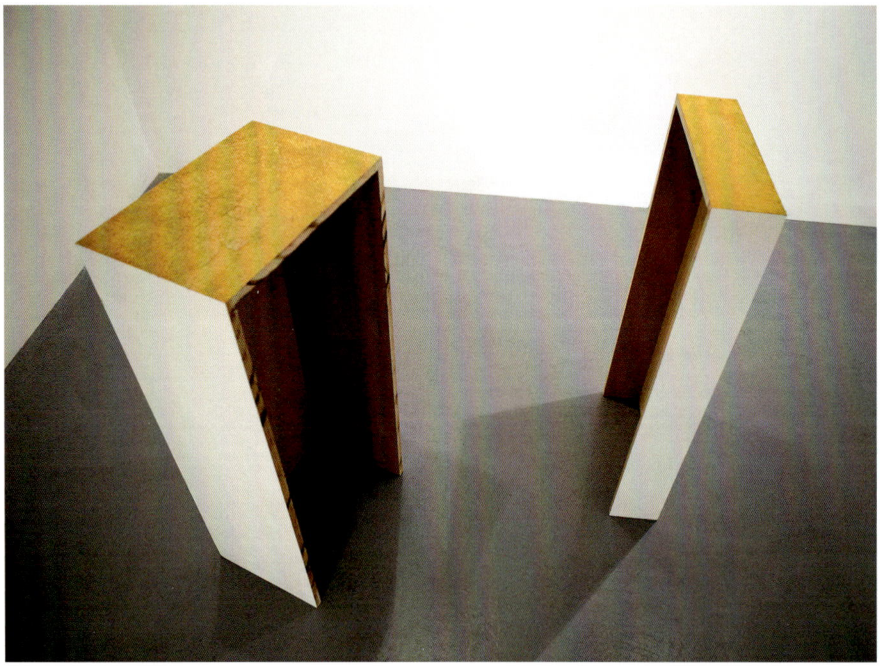

Sarah Bernhardt
Bee Pollen (2/3 Plinth)
Pigment (1/3 Plinth)
2013
Paint, MDF, bee pollen and pigment
39 3/8 x 17 11/16 x 12 3/16 in.
(100 x 45 x 31 cm) and
39 3/8 x 17 11/16 x 5 1/2 in.
(100 x 45 x 14 cm)

Martin John Callanan

Monday 18 March 2013; 15h00

Adriano Pedrosa: Why were you interested in participating in the project, why did you apply, and what are your expectations?
Martin John Callanan: I've shown in public galleries and festivals but hardly really in commercial galleries, so I'm interested to see how my works will function in that context.
And the fact that it's an open call?
I've never known a commercial gallery to have one, so I am interested in knowing what will happen.
How do you perceive this particular gallery in the larger context of London's art spaces?
It's definitely one of the top galleries in London and one that I have always visited. Having lived here since 2003 it's always been part of my London life and I have often gone to see what the shows were about.
Tell me about your work The Fundamental Units.
It's a work using coins of the lowest value sourced from every country in the world. By using the best microscope in Europe, at the National Physical Laboratory in Teddington, which takes 20,000 exposures of each coin's surface and recreates this photographic-like image, I was able to reveal all of the details.
Why do you say photographic-like?
It's not created using a camera. The lab uses a 3-D optical scanning microscope, which takes images from different angles and reconstructs it into a single image. We could call it a photograph as reflected light is captured, but it wasn't made with a camera. So far 16 of the 166 coins have been imaged.
You've made 16?

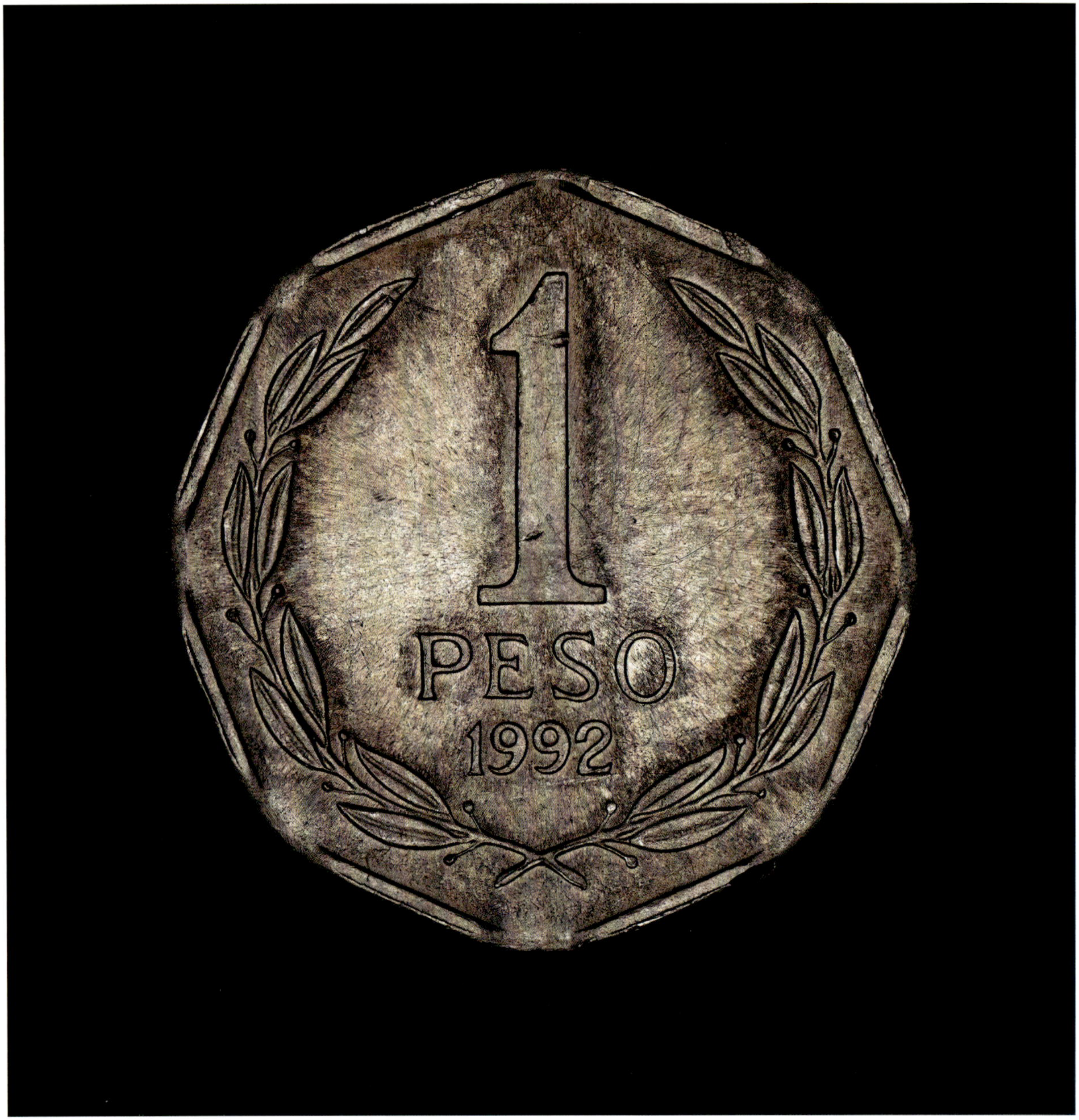
1
PESO
1992

Yes, and they are 1.2 metre prints in which you can see not only the wear and tear but also a hyper amount of detail. Detail that cannot normally be seen. You can even see how the coins were made in the foundry, like the stresses and the crystallization of the metal on the surface. It's trying to understand what money really is.
Which currencies have you worked with?
The project was partly funded by University College London's European Institute, so it's the 11 currencies in Europe plus Australia, Swaziland, Chile and Burma – one from each continent plus the European coins and Iceland.
Which is Europe as well?
Depends on which definition you use.
So the next step is to continue to look through other currencies until...
Until I have done all 166.
What would the next ones be? Do you have them already lined up?
I have all of the coins apart from two, which are proving quite hard to track down. They are Angola and the Island of Tuvalu – but there's some debate about whether they actually have coins or not, as they normally use the Australian currency, as those marked Tuvalu would appear to be solely commemorative and aimed at numismatists.
The coins are then printed against a black background?
Yes, and all 16 are available to view online.
Oh really, shall we look at that?
Sure. The website is *units.greyisgood.eu*
Oh you don't have Turkey though.
No.
Is Turkey not in Europe?
Not at the moment.
Is it the European Union or is it Europe?
It's Europe.
But there's a bit of it in Europe, no?
It wasn't on the list of European countries that I used.
Okay. It's one of those countries that half is and half isn't?
If you click on the coin itself it zooms right in, and you can see the detail if you keep clicking.
Wow.
So these are still at a low resolution compared to the prints, because

Martin John Callanan
The Fundamental Units (Chile)
2013
Photographic print
on dibond
47 1/4 x 47 1/4 in.
(120 x 120 cm)

they're online images.
Is this the scale at 1.2 metres?
It's almost the scale. These are a compressed version and the print would have...
Even more detail.
Absolutely.
How many times bigger are they?
They're 52 times bigger than the real coins, and the coins are relative to one another.
Are they expensive to produce?
Yes they are, but the National Physical Laboratory is kindly assisting me with the funding.
Have they been exhibited in London?
Not in London, but one was exhibited in Berlin.
Just one?
Yes, and five in Palma, Majorca last year.
They are framed with a grey wood?
Actually it's a black frame.
Is it very reflective?
Not especially. No more than a normal photograph.
But is there some plexi on top of it or something?
No, it's museum glass.
I see, museum, non-reflective glass?
Yes.

Martin John Callanan was born in 1982 in the UK and lives and works in London. He holds an MFA from the Slade School of Fine Art, London (2005) and is currently a Teaching Fellow, Fine Art Media, at the Slade School of Fine Art, London. Recent exhibitions include 'Along Some Sympathetic Lines', Or Gallery, Berlin (2013); Whitstable Biennale, UK (2012); Galeria Horrach Moya, Palma, Spain (2012) and 'Deed Poll' (performance), Whitechapel Gallery, London (2012).

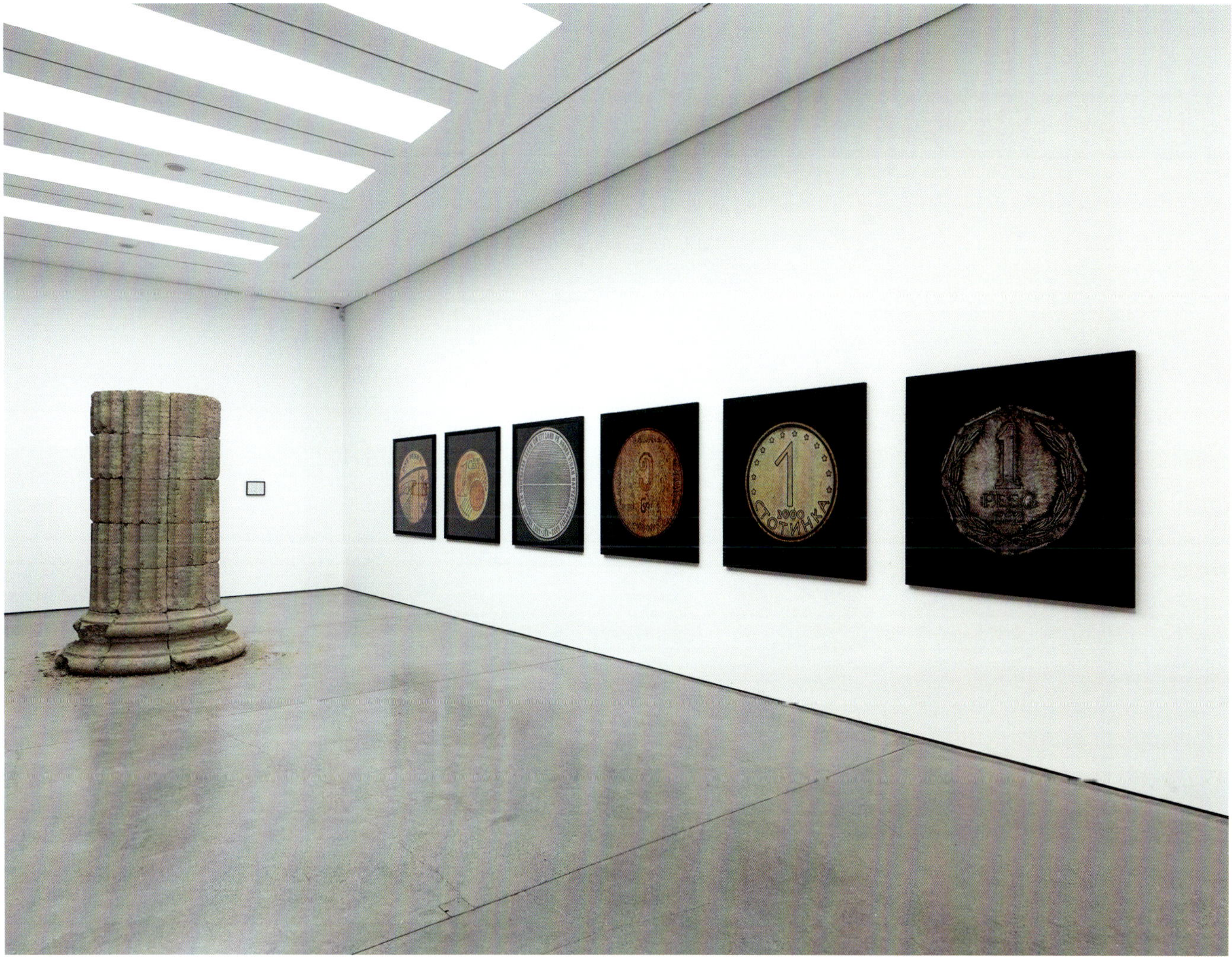
1
2000
СТОТИНКА
1
PESO

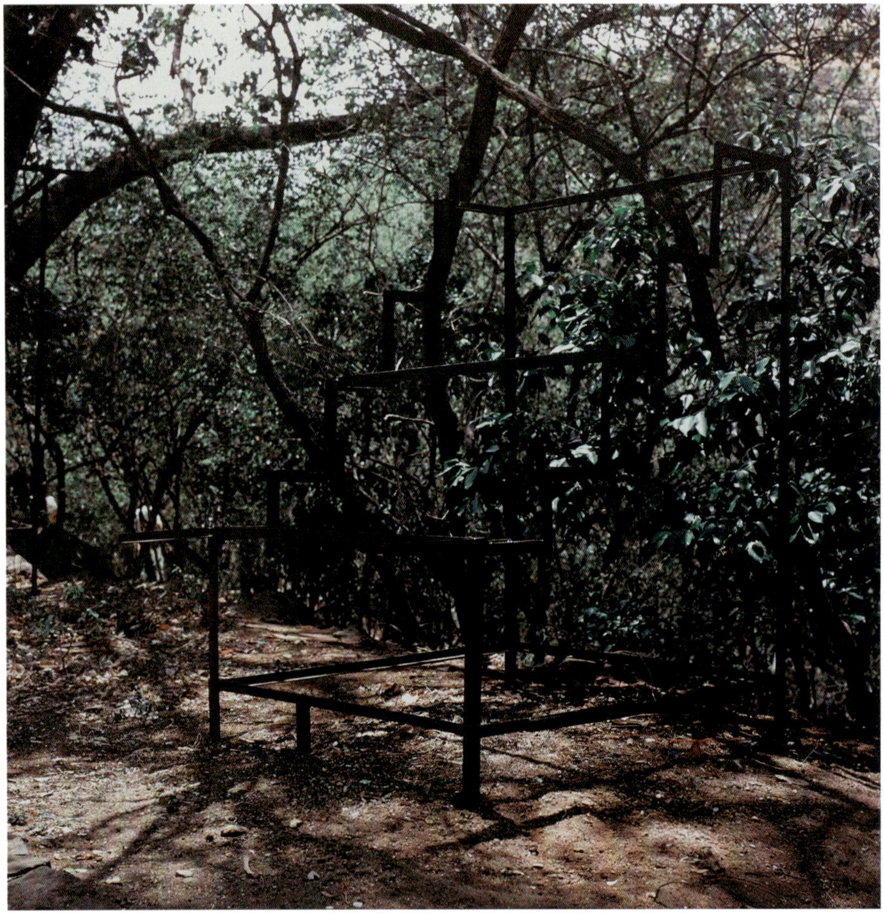

Nuno Direitinho
Untitled # 21 (Backbone)
2012
Digital print on dibond
23 5/8 x 23 5/8 in.
(60 x 60 cm)

Nuno Direitinho

Monday 18 March 2013; 11h30

Adriano Pedrosa: Before we start looking at images, I wanted to ask you why you applied and why you were interested in participating in the project, and exhibiting at White Cube.
Nuno Direitinho: I think it's a good opportunity, and the format is interesting, because there's a lot of things that aren't as relevant as in other applications. And providing 5 images of your work is quite a short submission.
What about White Cube in particular? And the open call? I proposed this project, which is an experiment with the gallery doing an open call, so I'm interested in hearing and learning from the artists about how they perceived it, and what led them to apply.
Are you asking me about the idea of the gallery, within the 'white space' and beyond the 'white space', as an 'open cube'?
Usually open calls are not from commercial galleries I believe, right? Like 'The London Open' at the Whitechapel or 'New Contemporaries', they're usually not commercial galleries, so how do you view a commercial gallery doing an open call then, as opposed to an institution? Does that make a difference for you?
I suppose it will make a difference, but I'm not sure that's one of my motivations for applying.
Well, here – it's a specific place, no? It's not like the 'white cube', which is completely dislocated from time and space. The gallery here is a very specific place, so I'm wondering whether you have an interest in this very specific place that White Cube is and where it positions itself. What are your thoughts about that?
It's kind of a landmark. I think as a gallery in London is in itself a thing and if...
The 'white cube' itself, the model of the traditional 'white cube', which is

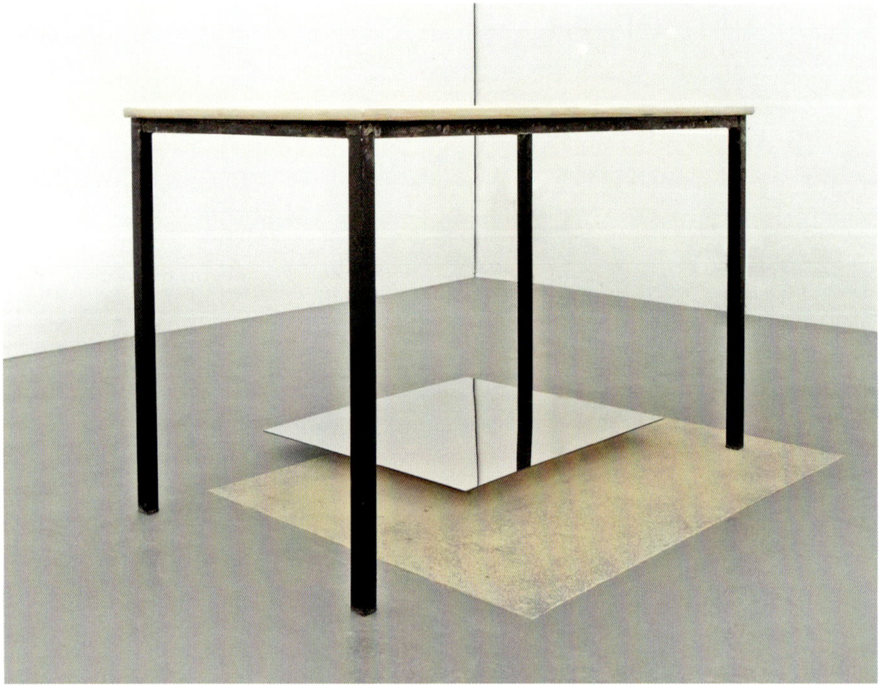

detached from history, from space, timeless, above everything else, doesn't really exist. Everything is contaminated with many things that surround it, whether it's London or the courtyard outside, or the business that is done here, or the types of artists that are exhibited. Did you considered any of that when you applied?
I suppose it's just very hard for me to grasp that notion before the fact.
Okay, Let's look at Dialogue on Tides, *from 2012. Can you tell me something about this work?*
First of all I think I should say that I come from a photography background having trained in photography before I attended the Slade, and one of the things I've been trying to do with my work is to push it further and blend it into some of the objects, ideas and concepts that were in the photographs I took before, so that they can somehow become the reverse of the photographs. So that when you encounter them you are not encountering something that belongs to another moment, is an experience of another moment, but is more

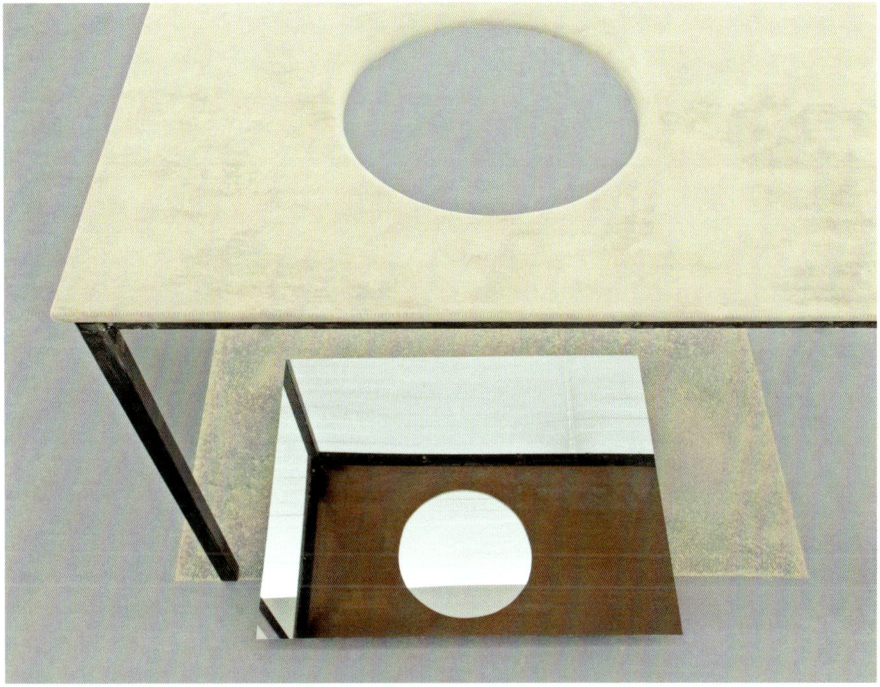

of a reflection of the current moment. Does that make sense?
It does make sense. There is a photographic element here somewhere?
In the sense of its concept and composition – for me it is very much a photographic composition and it acts as a photograph and as an image-making device, which is how I view a photograph. With this work I've sanded down the top of the table and used the sawdust to make the rectangle on the floor, and then the mirror is placed on top of the sawdust.
How is the mirror suspended? Is there something propping it up off the floor?
It's standing on its own small wooden stand. Trying to be invisible.
Where was it exhibited?
At the Slade, quite recently.
Last year, right?
Yes.
Is this related to any other previous works of yours somehow?

Nuno Direitinho
Dialogue on Tides
2012
Wood, metal, mirror and sanding dust
31 1/2 x 27 15/16 x 48 1/16 in.
(80 x 71 x 122 cm)

It's related to my more recent works. For a long time now I've been trying to create an image by reducing the concept, so I have a set of objects, or I have a set of ideas, and then I try to remove some until I can get to a point where the ideas or the concept make sense.

Is this work a slide projection?

Yes, and the work is titled *A pause in looking*, from 2012. There are 72 slides on 80 slide holders, so there are gaps in-between. The images are of seascapes taken from above, looking down onto the sea, and it's generally to do with the idea of blinking and trying to compress memories into slides.

When one blinks?

The photograph becomes a metaphor for the concept of the space in-between thinking or the space in-between pieces of information.

But this is quite photographic.

Yes.

Did you take the photographs or did you appropriate them?

I took the photographs.

Did you fly over the ocean?

No, I was on the top of a cliff.

But they're black and white, do they really read as images of water?

I think they do.

I can't tell because here it just seems like it could be an abstraction somehow. It almost seems like gestural brush strokes.

I think it's partly because I've kept them reversed, so they're negatives. They are projected as negatives.

I see. It does relate to Dialogue on Tides.

Nuno Direitinho was born in 1981 in Portugal and lives and works in London. He holds a BA in Fine Art Photography from Glasgow School of Art, Glasgow (2011), and is currently doing his MFA in Fine Art Media at the Slade School of Fine Art, London. Recent exhibitions include 'Voies Off', La Galerie à Ciel Ouvert, Arles, France (2012); 'Emergentes DST', Teatro Circo, Braga, Portugal (2011) and '3+1', Assembly Gallery, Glasgow (2011).

Venisha Francis-Hinkson

Monday 18 March 2013; 12h30

Adriano Pedrosa: I wanted to ask you why you were interested in participating, why you applied and what kind of expectations you have?
Venisha Francis-Hinkson: White Cube is such a name and to be a part of that is an amazing opportunity for me and for my practice. I mean White Cube, I can't even express it to be honest.
How do you perceive the gallery?
It's dream for me.
A dream!
I'm speechless.
Well thank you so much for coming. I really appreciate it.
The actual artwork is the spools, which is a transcript of dialogue from the film *Bring it On*, that I've painstakingly scratched onto the surface of the videotape. The unit is just a way of allowing the viewer to read the dialogue as it goes around.
I'm sorry, I'm not familiar with the film.
It's a really cheesy American film starring Kirsten Dunst, it's like a chick-flick about cheerleaders. At the time I had the idea I was rummaging through VHSs I had at home, and that film was the one whose dialogue I could remember and I thought, 'It's quite universal', so despite not knowing the film you'll see little bits of it and sort of relate to it and have a laugh with it. The beauty of it is that it can be any film, so it doesn't necessarily need be a film that *I've* made.
Did you do this for an exhibition?
Yes, this was my degree show piece for Camberwell College of Art.
Are people supposed to interact with this?
It can be an interactive piece. It was interesting just to watch how

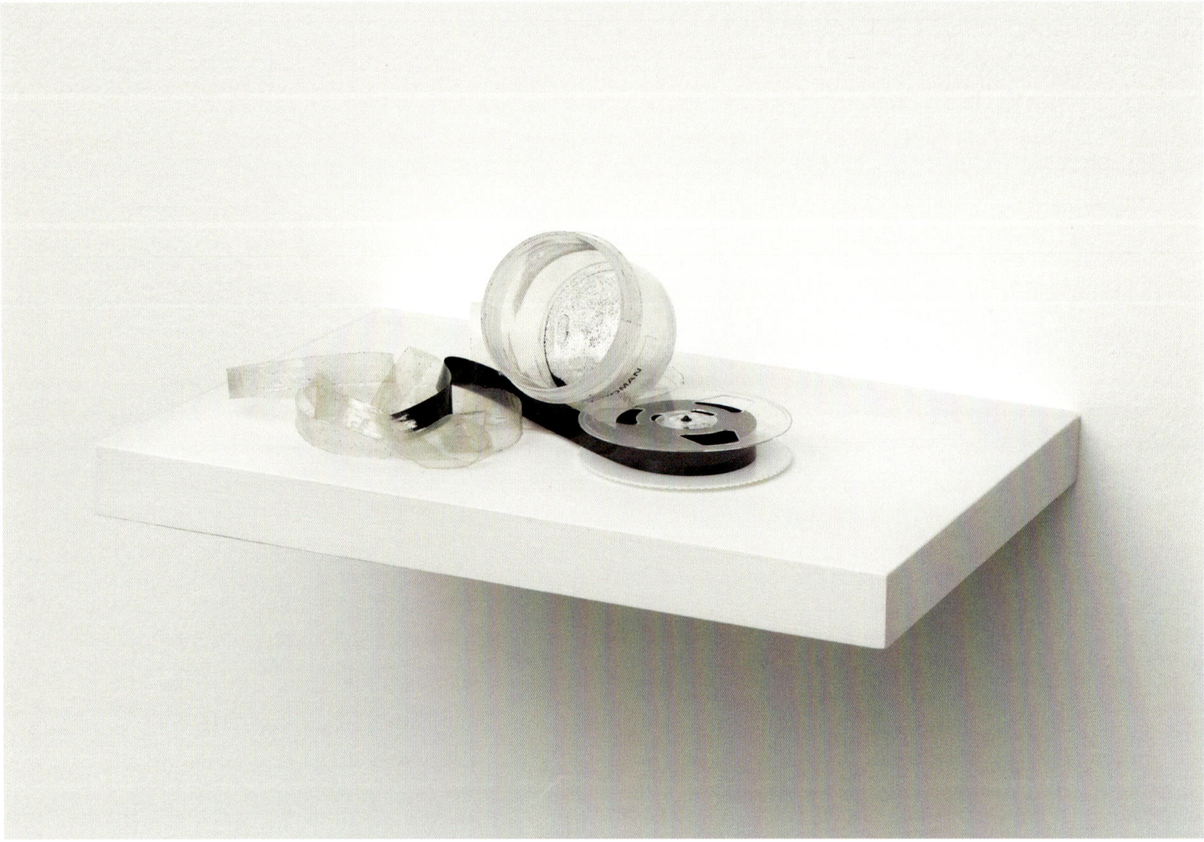

Venisha Francis-Hinkson
Erasure
2011
Videotape and container
Dimensions variable

people engaged with it.
Is it one scene?
For the moment, yes.
It describes it?
No, I went online and I found the dialogue of the film and then scratched it onto the surface of the videotape.
The entire videotape?
To be honest, I'm still working on it, so it's a piece I'm still finishing, a work in progress.
Ideally it would use the entire film?
Yes.
All scratched?
Yes, and it's also the actual spools of the video itself.
Oh right.
I've also brought along *Erasure*, which is the film *Pretty Woman*. I've scratched away the surface of the film and stored the ashes in a container, which sort of becomes the artwork itself.
You didn't send an image of this one did you?
Yes, but the image looks quite different.
Was that work also in your graduation show?
No, this piece, *Script*, was for my graduation show.
Just this piece?
Yes, just this piece.
Was it a group show?
Yes.
But was this exhibited in its own space?
No, it was exhibited among other artists' works, but because of the way it was designed it needed more space to breathe, because it's quite an intimate piece.
So the film itself, you said possibly it could be used with other films?
Yes, I titled the work *Script* so that other films could be played.
Bring it On, *do you know the release date of that film?*
2000, and it was directed by Peyton Reed.
Can you write it down for me? I know it's a 'chick-flick', which is a film popular with women supposedly. But each film would bring a completely different context, so why were you interested in the context of this film in particular?
Because at the time I came up with the idea, that was the film I had,

I could relate to it and also found it quite funny.

And Pretty Woman*? Why did you choose that film?*

I just thought that this violent act of scratching away the surface of the videotape considering that the film is called *Pretty Woman*, is both comical and poetic.

Is there a feminist sub-text?

My practice does suggest that, as I crochet, stitch and knit cassette and videotape. But I wouldn't say so, no.

Subtexts can be very far fetched.

These two pieces don't have to be exhibited together; they can be exhibited independently of one another.

But what does it mean to erase a film? It's almost like you can read it as if it were a portrait of a 'pretty woman', no? So here you have an erased pretty woman. What is the character in that film? I haven't seen it in a long time so what does that character represent? Of course it's the film title, but do you also think that she doesn't have a name, that she is supposedly identified by her most defining characteristic – that of a 'pretty' woman. That's why I'm reading a possible feminist subtext into it. Does that make sense?

Yes.

Those are the areas that I'm interested in, and we each bring our own interests and perspectives to a work.

When I make a work the things I think of when I'm making it, and how I interpret it, are completely different to how I would have thought of it. Each artwork has different possible interpretations. With *Script*, I'm more concerned with the immediacy of cinema and that it's almost like you're watching a film – but actually you're *reading* the film. The thing I was getting from it was that people interpret it differently when they read it.

Perhaps the next level here in this piece, Script*, is its metalinguistic quality, as it deals not only with the image but also the text, how that's represented and portrayed, and how that becomes an artwork. It's quite conceptual in that sense, because you're scratching words, so that as you scratch the words you are also erasing the film which is represented through this, I guess, outdated technology? Even though VHS is outdated, a representation is still somehow scripted there, so this metalinguistic play could possibly be brought onto another level, or unfolded into a, perhaps, more complex way through the choice of film. Of course, you can apply it to any film but each film would bring a very different*

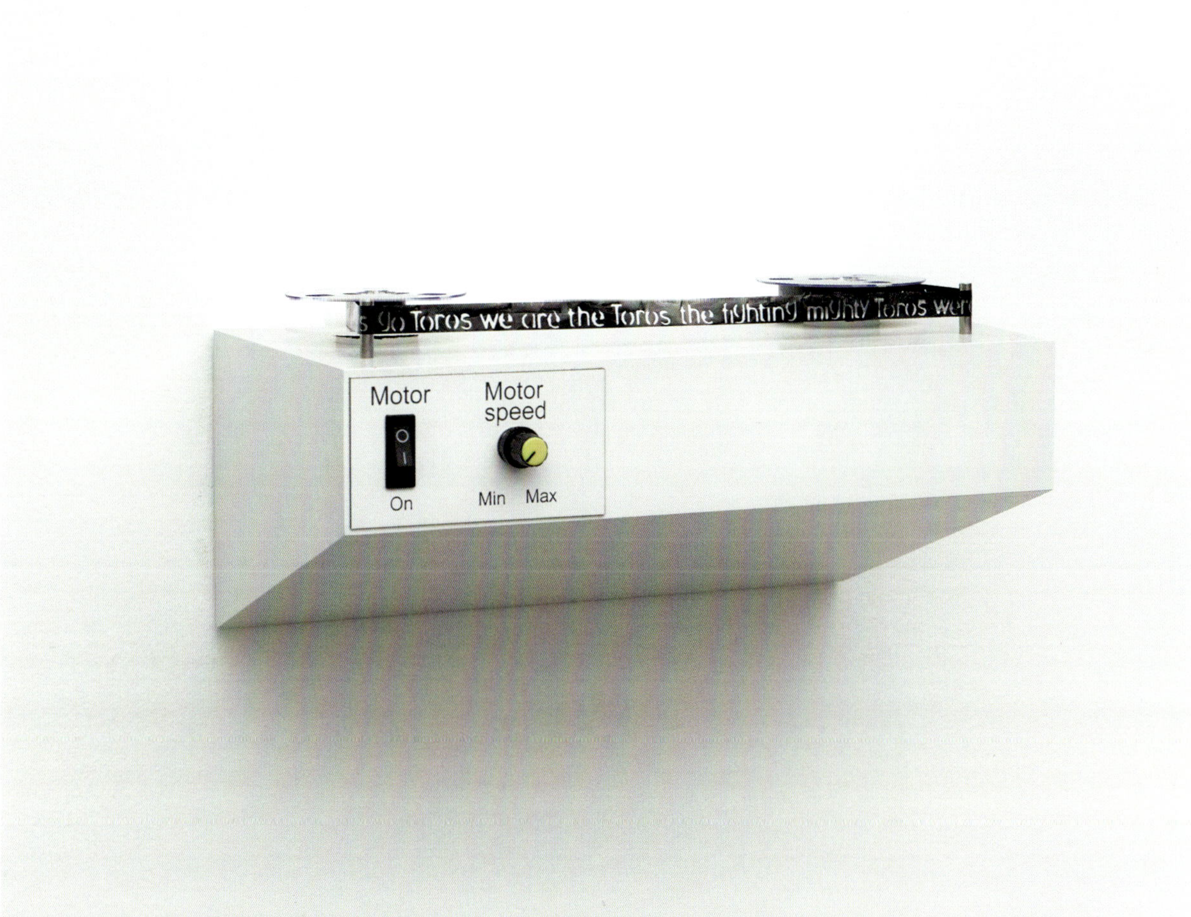

Venisha Francis-Hinkson
Script
2012
Videotape
Dimensions variable

story, so perhaps that's another possibility for exploring the work further. Have you erased and done these operations with any other films?

No, I haven't, but with this one, because time is something that is in my work a lot, time becomes part of the work as well. And like you say, I'm really interested in this redundant material. I don't know what it is about the material, it just interests and excites me. It's like I'm a child who wants to play and do all these things, and I've got a whole diary of things that I haven't...

Oh, you are still working on Pretty Woman*?*

Yes.

Oh, so this is just a section of Pretty Woman*?*

It's such an arduous process, but there are other projects that I have on the go at the same time, which are equally arduous.

Venisha Francis-Hinkson was born in 1989 in England and lives and works in London. She holds a BTEC National Diploma in Art and Design from St. Francis Xavier College (2009) and a BA (Hons) in Drawing from Camberwell College of Arts (2012). Recent exhibitions include 'Future Map 12', CSM Lethaby & Window Galleries, London (2013); The Learning Resource Centre, Camberwell College of Arts (2012) and 'Peek Show', The Biscuit Factory, London (2011).

Rodrigo Garcia Dutra

Saturday 16 March 2013; 17h00

Adriano Pedrosa: Why were you interested in participating in this project?
Rodrigo Garcia Dutra: I think it's good to establish a relationship with an English institution. Coming from Brazil, and having shown mostly in Brazil and other countries, I don't have much presence here, so it's a good way to present myself whilst I am studying here. I think it's important to establish a relationship with English galleries and the English circuit and to not just go back to Brazil without having done that. When you're in school people tend to look for networks to find their way, and this is a better way to do it. You don't only have to go networking, you can also do applications, or make proposals, which is good for artists.
And what about White Cube itself, how do you perceive the gallery?
I've seen many exhibitions at the Hoxton space, because that's where I used to live. I think it's a great gallery and has this big profile which I don't think I fit into so much. Still, there is space for young artists to show work here. There's a new White Cube in São Paulo, which I haven't had an opportunity to see, but I find that really interesting, in terms of the relationship with São Paulo. It says a lot about what a 'Brave New World' we are living in. There's a new kind of dynamic happening.
And why do you say you don't relate so much to the gallery?
I think there is a blue-chip artist's situation here. I think I'm quite young, I'm 32. I know there are young artists working with White Cube already, but I see myself working with a smaller gallery, a different kind of place.
This is a single piece that we're looking at?

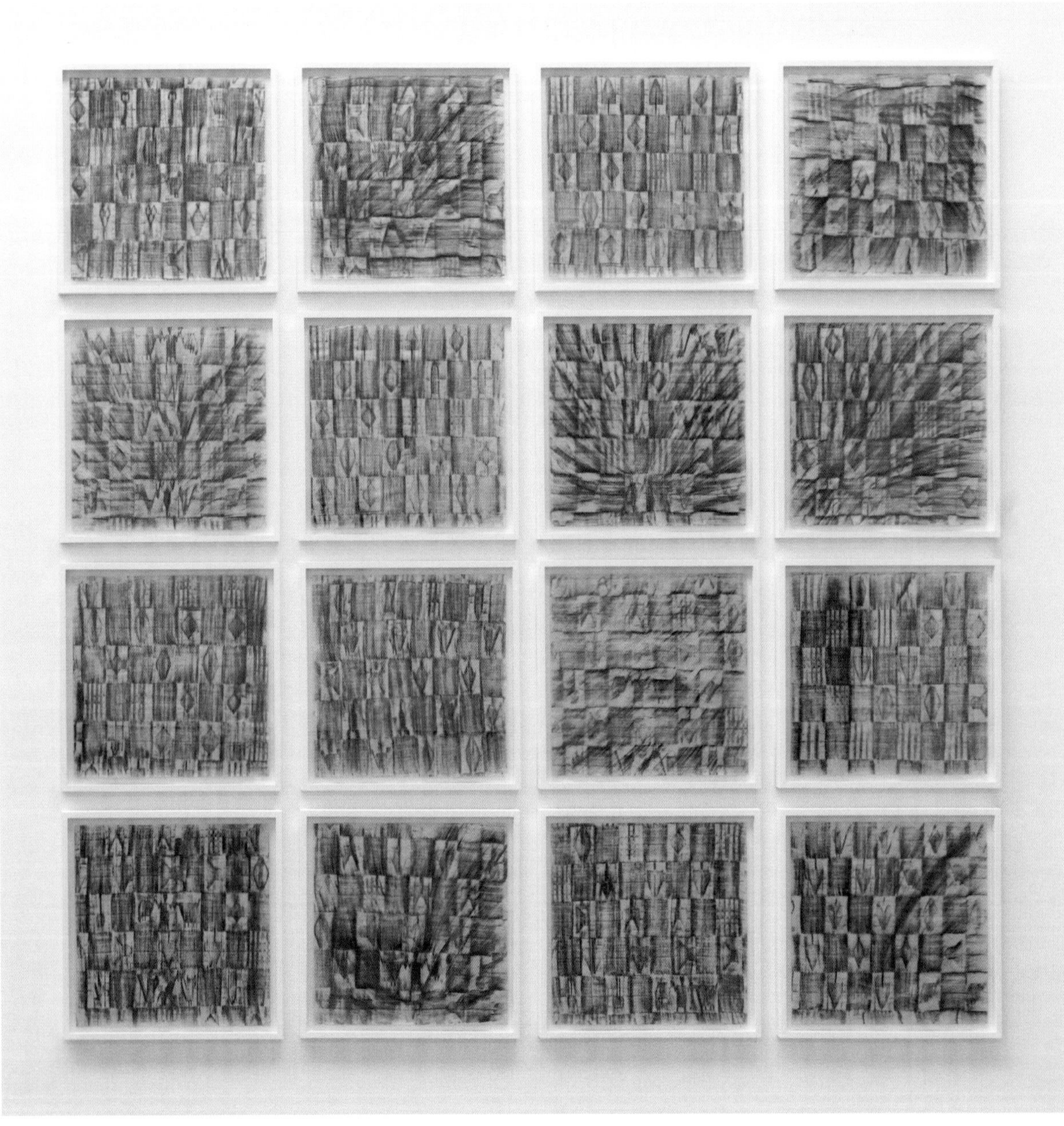

Yes.
And then you have the African textiles, which are?
It's a present. Someone saw this, thought of me and gave me the textile and this book, *Building on a Construct: The Adolpho Leirner Collection of Brazilian Constructive Art at the Museum of Fine Arts, Houston.*
Where does the textile come from?
West Africa. From the Ewe people.
Have you been looking at African textiles, or is it your first encounter?
This one I looked at because it was a present, and then I looked at other ones on the internet. It's on Wikipedia, and you can find more examples. The most intriguing thing was that someone thought of me when they saw this aesthetic. Then, I took the 'shadow' of these textiles. I did the frottage in charcoal.
How did you receive this gift, which seems like it has an abstract geometric composition and is very colourful? And how did you place that in juxtaposition to the book on the Adolpho Leirner collection?
First of all, this form started to mean something to me after I thought about the origins of Brazilian Constructivism and Neo-Concretism, related to the European avant-garde myth, being itself inspired by tribal motifs from older civilizations. I'm interested in the origin of things and how form travels in space and time, and how the form acquires different meanings through this journey. So in this present, in this moment, to be remembered through this and to be given it was quite meaningful for me. It was about my personal interests.
What is the connection that you are trying to make through this juxtaposition of the Adolpho Leirner Collection of Brazilian Constructive Art and the African textiles?
To trace the origins of my own interests in this kind of language.
Do you think there was a connection between Brazilian Constructivist art and African textiles?
Clearly!
You think there was?
Yes, through the African immigrants in Brazil.
But can you trace that in the work or is it something that you are making up yourself?
No, I'm not making it up, but it's like when you 'suppose' something.
But have you read that anywhere?

Rodrigo Garcia Dutra
When in dead night thy fair imperfect shade I–XVI
2013
Charcoal on paper
Each: 19 11/16 x 19 11/16 in. (50 x 50 cm)

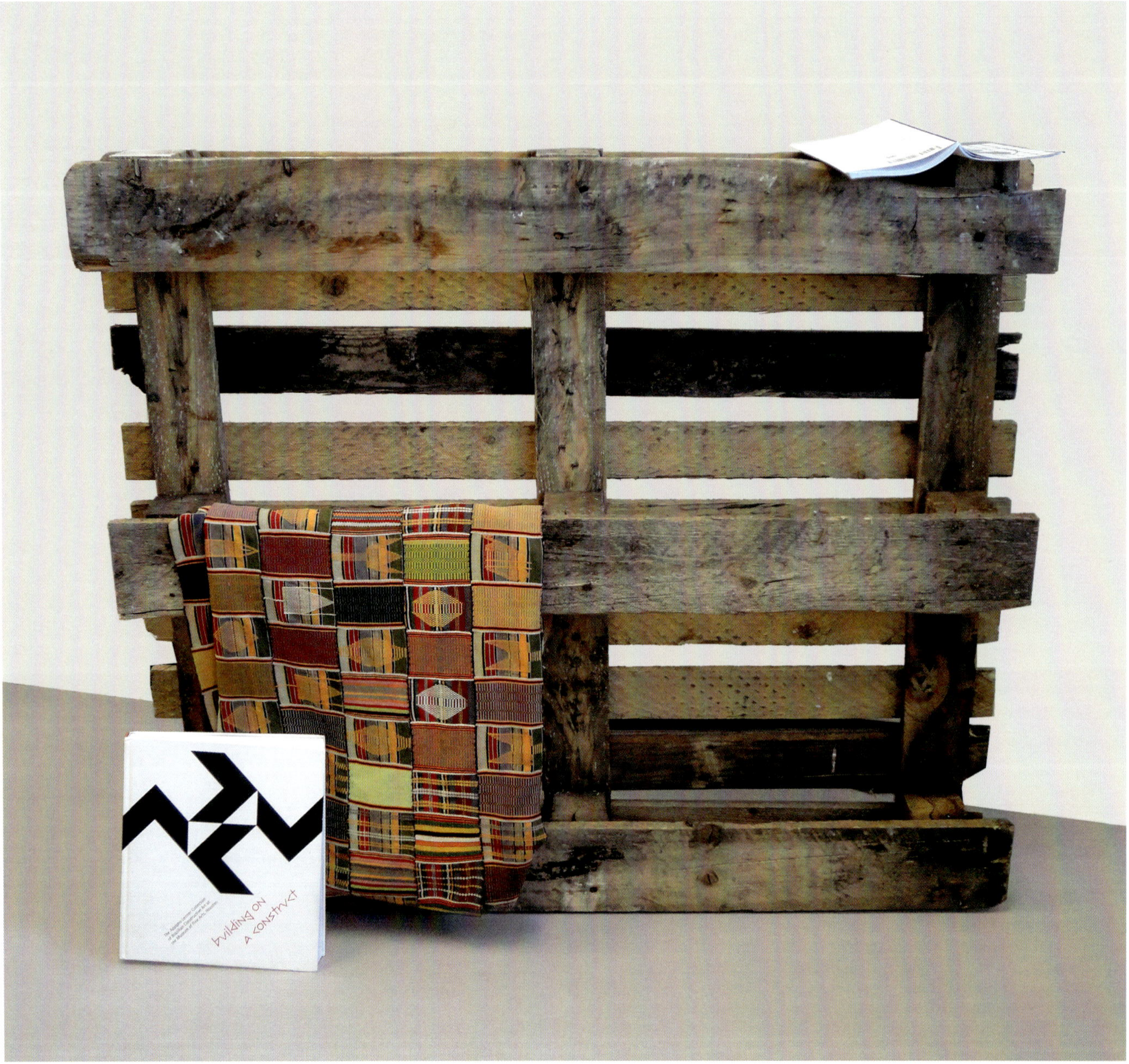
building on
a construct

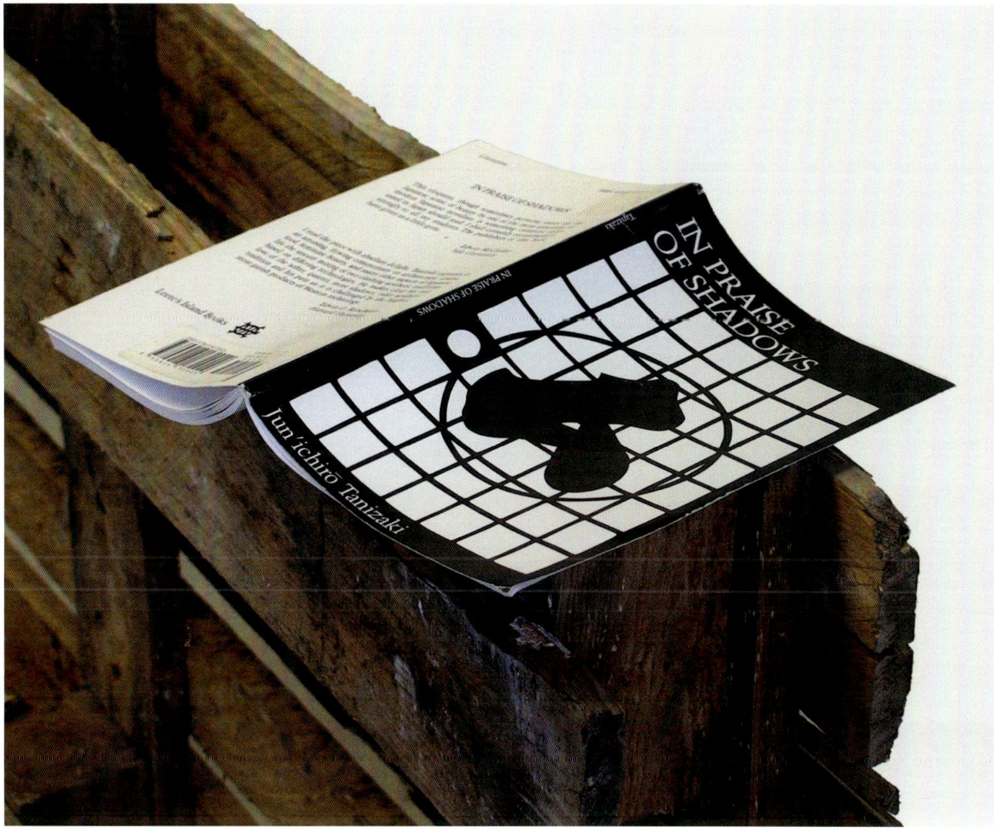

Rodrigo Garcia Dutra
Tabom
2013
Wooden pallet, textile
and books
39 3/8 x 47 1/4 x 15 3/4 in.
(100 x 120 x 40 cm)

No. But it's clear. I think it's clear.

What, through the images?

No, through other artists that work with it. I've forgotten his name, he was from Salvador.

Rubem Valentim?

Yes, to me it's very clear that some of it originates from that. It's obvious actually, you can tell.

I wish it was.

You wish?

I would love to but I don't think it is. I've actually been researching those connections and trying to make up the connections. I don't think historically they were there.

As an artist I find it very interesting how you can intuitively use fiction to say something about reality – it's not about being accurate.

What about the wooden palette?

It is a sculpture or it transports sculpture – it's this idea of using a palette on which to place this textile and the book. There is a book about Japanese aesthetics. It talks a lot about toilets and how Japanese toilets are made to be used in the dark, so during the darkness you can see the beauty of its patterns.

Just one second, there are a few elements here that are of interest I feel: it's a grid, it's constructivist, geometric. It's horizontals and verticals, you can see it in a Constructive way. There is a young artist in South Africa also working with crates.

With this object?

Yes, Serge Alain Nitegeka, he also paints them. Anyhow it's also an object used to transport things back and forth, and what you're doing here is transporting ideas and histories.

Aesthetics and styles.

So it makes sense when you're bridging the Brazilian with the West African and the Japanese, in that sense.

And England. That's where it's located. I was doing this research about this Imperial Palace in Japan which is the source of the International Style of architecture.

I read that, do you have that book here?

Yes.

I'm also curious how this relates to all this. Are these two separate pieces?

They are separate pieces but they are together in the space; it's a work in progress.
I see, alright, I was trying to understand how they all came together.
But I think all artists, all works are 'in progress' in a way.
At some point they get bought.
Yes, a fair point.
It's gone and you can't change it.
Yes, but I think these connections are being established through time.
So In Praise of Shadows, *what is this?*
It's a book about Japanese aesthetics but basically about darkness, because Japanese aesthetics were built around darkness. When they didn't have electric light, everything would be lit by candles and everything would have to be visible in the dark. All the textures, all the details, were subtly revealed by the lighting of candles, which is not present in this work, but as I work with video projections as well, I'm also interested in this contrast between light and darkness, and the Shakespeare sonnet is all about this.
What does it mean to do a frottage of an African textile?
Its appearance becomes a shadow again, as with a sculpture, where you make a bronze casting of a person and you keep this identity 'alive'. This frottage gives a new ghostly appearance of that object; it's not colourful anymore, it's black and white. It's a translation and when you translate something into another medium it's always a betrayal because you are betraying the original qualities of the object.
It's a beautiful object. It's a great idea because what you do is render it in black and white, you render it graphic, Concrete.
Yes, and it also connects to that picture you have of those Indians, those native Brazilians.
By Debret.
I'm a native Brazilian as well.
We all are now.

Rodrigo Garcia Dutra was born in 1981 in Rio de Janeiro, Brazil and lives and works in London. He holds an MA Fine Art from Central Saint Martin's College of Art and Design, London (2009) and is currently studying for an MA in Sculpture at the Royal College of Art, London. In 2010 he was awarded the Fundação Bienal de São Paulo, Programa Brasil Arte Contemporânea. Recent exhibitions include 'Notes to Self', Royal College of Art, London (2013); 'Outras Coisas Visiveis Sobre Papel', Galerie Leme, São Paulo (2012); 'Theory of the City or the Possibilities of an A4', ISCP, New York City, USA (2011) and '17 Ingredients: Measures of Autonomy', BASH Studios, London (2009).

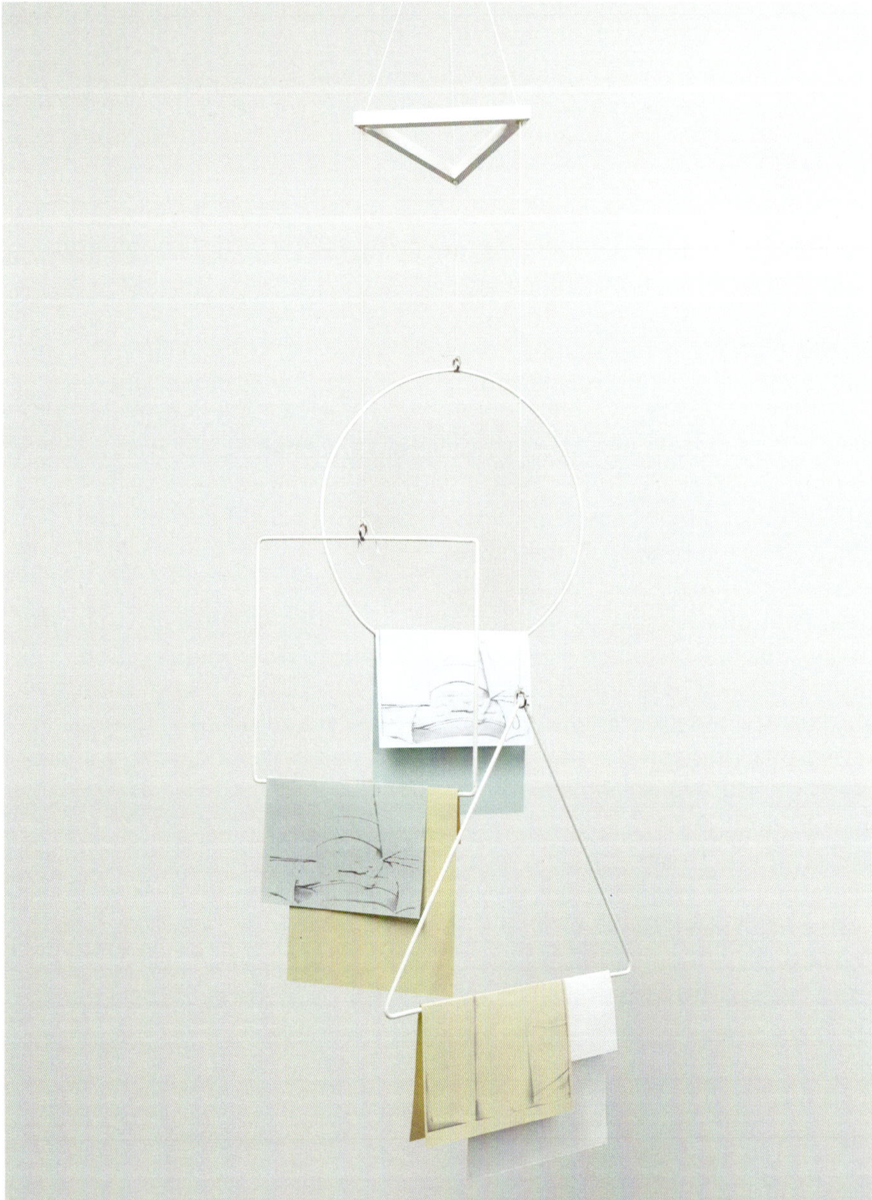

Rowena Harris

Sunday 17 March 2013; 15h30

Adriano Pedrosa: Could you tell me why you are interested in participating in the project and why you applied?
Rowena Harris: I think it's interesting for White Cube to do an open submission, and I think it's unusual for a gallery of this size to do something of that nature. Open submissions can often be interesting as you never know where you're at, but with White Cube I'd imagine the selection process will be refined, and you might have a particular objective for selecting the work. With other open submissions there may not be a theme, but I thought that White Cube would do something that's more interesting.
And how do you see the gallery itself, its position and its role in the London scene?
I guess it has a good selection of very established artists, and does very interesting shows. In comparison to Saatchi Gallery which seems to be much more about a very particular aesthetic or trend or work that's quite eye-catching, whereas some of the exhibitions at White Cube are investigating something quite exploratory and White Cube provides the space for artists to do something interesting.
Tell me about this work.
This is a work in three parts. I think about paper as this thing between the digital and the material, and trying to bring about a gesture that has a relationship with the body in opposition to digital experience. I want the viewer to experience the gesture as a physical memory, so I selected t-shirts because they have this physical memory of being worn – a distinct relationship to the body. I then folded them into an A4 size and coated them with layers of paint, which you can see renders them very tactile.

Rowena Harris
Accreted Part 2
2012
Paper, photocopy, steel, enamel and nylon
27 9/16 x 17 11/16 x 13 3/4 in.
(70 x 45 x 35 cm)

Did you use acrylic paint?
No, emulsion paint, which makes them matt and brittle. Then I stacked them on top of each other. I was playing with this idea of compression, which is not only a digital term for making files smaller but it's also a material term and a gesture, something you can feel. I wanted to look at the relationship between the digital use of that term and the material use of that term, so I wanted to make the t-shirts seem squashed and paper-like and have them compressed in a pile.
There are about 6 t-shirts?
There are more in the white pile which is a bit larger. You can still see the form of the t-shirt through the paint but the fabric is definitely saturated.
It looks like plaster, no?
Yes, they seem to be casts of t-shirts.
You can still recognise them from here it seems. And they are just balancing, one on top of the other, so the equilibrium is rather fragile.
It's fragile and they will fall over if they are lent against. But surprisingly they are reasonably stable and they're actually quite heavy.
Can you tell me something about Accreted Part 2*?*
This is a photo of part 2 of the same work which comprises photocopies of the folded t-shirts, printed onto similar coloured paper.
I see you are using the triangle, the circle and the square.
Which is like Bauhaus.
Yes.
I want to say that this is a 'sculpture-sculpture' and…
It's not a good quality image really, but I understand.
I guess it's the translation of the t-shirt sculptures into a paper medium.
It hangs from the ceiling?
Yes.
At about eye height?
Maybe with this one, yes. I think it's about eye height.
So it's a kind of mobile really. It's in the centre of the space. For some reason I thought it was more towards the wall, but it's not.
It is closer to the wall in the photograph than I'd like it to be.
Oh okay, but it's supposed to be something that you…?
Walk around.
And then there is this play again with the modernist idioms?

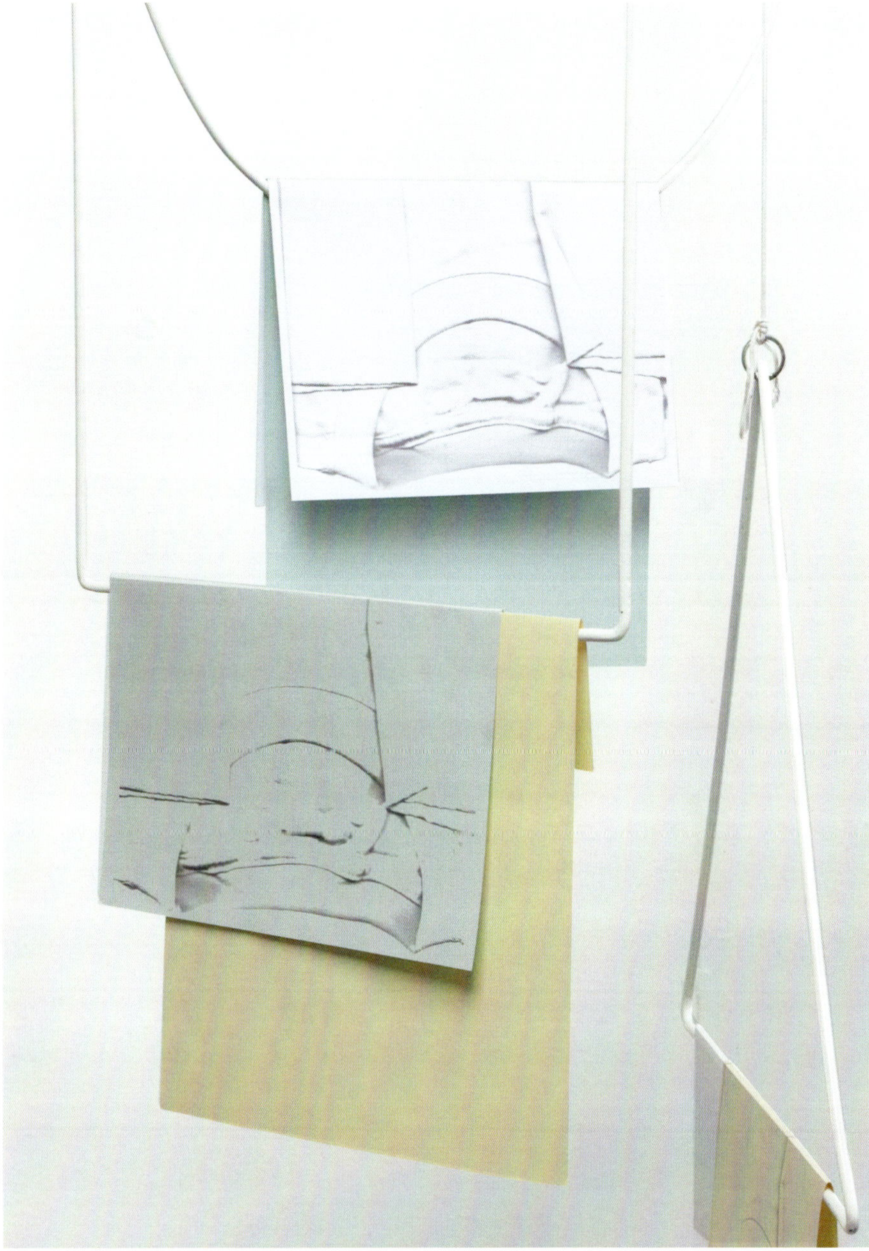

Rowena Harris
Accreted Part 2 (detail)
2012
Paper, photocopy, steel, enamel and nylon
27 9/16 x 17 11/16 x 13 3/4 in.
(70 x 45 x 35 cm)

Yes.
And here, with geometric abstraction?
I think it's a reference really.
Well a play at least. You are playing with it, no?
Yes.
You're not completely invested in it because you have these representations of representations of representations of bodies or, in a metonymic way, the body is close to the t-shirt and then it's plastered and photocopied and folded, there is a play between the 3-dimensional and 2-dimensional, the photographic and the sculptural, as well as the see-through.
That's what I was looking for, many different translations of what it could be.
What about the colour scheme?
It's yellow, blue and white.
Is that colour blue?
It's sort of bluish-green. They are paper colours, and oddly enough when I painted the t-shirts, white didn't look like paper.
Those colours are not very close to the palette of classic, geometric abstraction.
Absolutely not, definitely not – but they are like paper.
They are more like baby colours, pale colours, pastel colours. Do you think the two parts are supposed to be exhibited together?
I think they can exist apart, but I think the total understanding comes from them being together, but I'm interested in their understanding being determined from the various ways one might find them, over a longer period of time and in different places. Different exhibitions perhaps and in documentation.
It seems a bit didactic to have one next to each other, and almost seems like step 1, step 2, and then I wonder what step 3 is?
It's a bit of a wacky one. It's entirely digital and only available online.

Rowena Harris was born in 1985 in Norfolk and lives and works in London. She holds a BA in Fine Art from University College Falmouth, UK (2008) and an MFA Art Practice from Goldsmiths College, London (2010). She is the founder and editor of a bi-annual art publication, Misery Connoisseur. Her recent solo exhibition was 'Believing in Things', Van Horbourg Gallery, Basel (2011), and group exhibitions include 'Cold Compress', Drei Gallery, Cologne (2012); 'No More Icons', Rod Barton Gallery, London (2012) and 'New Contemporaries', ICA, London and at the A Foundation, Liverpool (2010).

Alan Magee

Saturday 16 March 2013; 11h00

Adriano Pedrosa: Why were you interested in participating in this project?
Alan Magee: Because it's going to be a great opportunity to have my work seen by a new audience and to show with some, probably, really exciting people that I have not shown with before, and then obviously to have a more international perspective on the work from yourself, and the other curators that are involved, as I'm sure it was a big team initially.
Oh, it's just me.
Just you?
Yes!
My goodness.
Just me. I mean, of course the team here looks through it with me, but in terms of the curatorial selection, it's just me.
Wow, that must have been a serious task.
Yes.
And so obviously there's White Cube. It's almost an institution in itself, so you know, showing work here would be a great validation of my practice which would be really, really nice – a nice boost, and then hopefully to initiate some dialogues with the other artists, and to realise some other opportunities out of the show.
It's interesting that you say that it's almost like an institution; it's my first time in here. Of course I know the gallery, but I don't live here, so I don't get much of a sense of the position and the role the gallery has in the London scene. How do you see the position of the gallery in terms of the art scene, not just the gallery scene, but in terms of the art scene in general?
In terms of the art scene?

What role does the gallery play?
London has been a very interesting experience for me. I've only been here for five years, and previously a lot of my exposure to the 'classics' of art had been through documentation. So when I came here there was this amazing sense of opportunity, that I could see these works in the real, which was something quite huge for me. There's a certain level of blue-chip artist that is shown here, and pretty much everybody that White Cube represents is of that standard. I'd never had that much of an opportunity before to see them.
Do you think that the gallery plays a different, complimentary or distinct role in terms of the larger institutional thing?
Well, galleries have a remit, and they tend to show artists who might, you know, not to be ungenerous, but who might make more money for the gallery. But then there are the slightly more fringe artists, who will be pushing the boundaries a little bit. That's always quite nice to see, how they co-exist in the same space, and how they occupy different roles.
Here at White Cube?
Yes, at White Cube, and I guess Lisson Gallery has similar standards and a similar spread of artists, but most galleries have that. So it's lovely to see somebody having the room to do what they want to do with slightly less financial constraints. It's a different remit for other institutions I think, like your Tate's and your museums. I guess they have more of an educational role; they're influenced by what they do in that sense. By contrast, White Cube, I presume, has a bit of freedom, a bit of autonomy, so that it can spearhead something – it can make decisions and be less accountable to a 'committee', so-to-speak.
You went to school at St Martins, no?
Yes, that's right.
When did you graduate from there?
I studied there from 2008 to 2009.
I was curious about Veneered Off-Cuts. *Can you tell me a little bit about that work? Were you able to bring any of the elements with you?*
Yes I brought two of the offcuts. You can see that this work brings together a number of different elements that I was investigating. There are obvious connections between use, value and function, in so far as this piece is concerned. For example, one of the offcuts was also

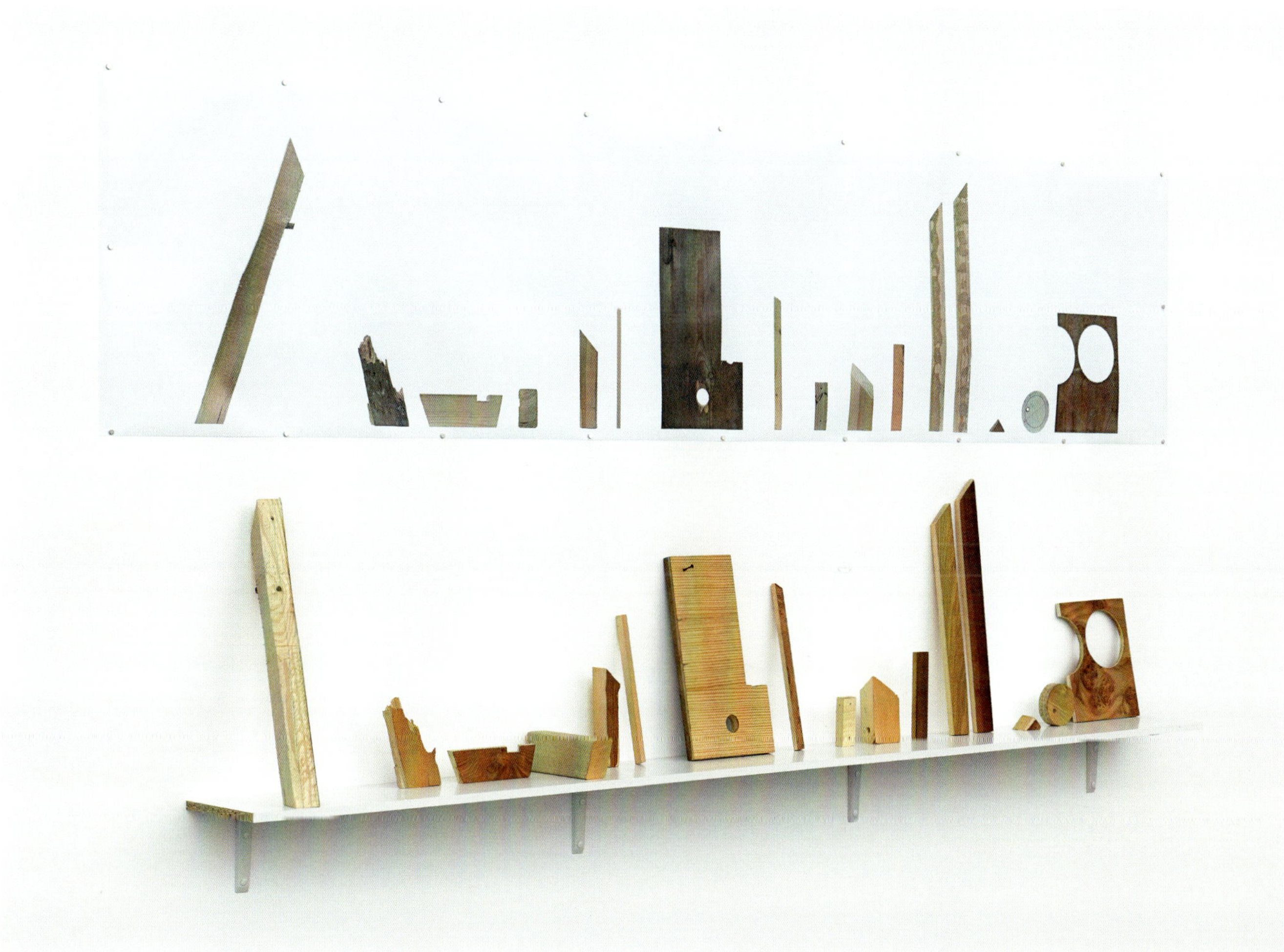

Alan Magee
Veneered Off-Cuts
2011
Wood, shelf and photographic print
48 1/16 x 108 11/16 x 9 1/16 in.
(122 x 276 x 23 cm)

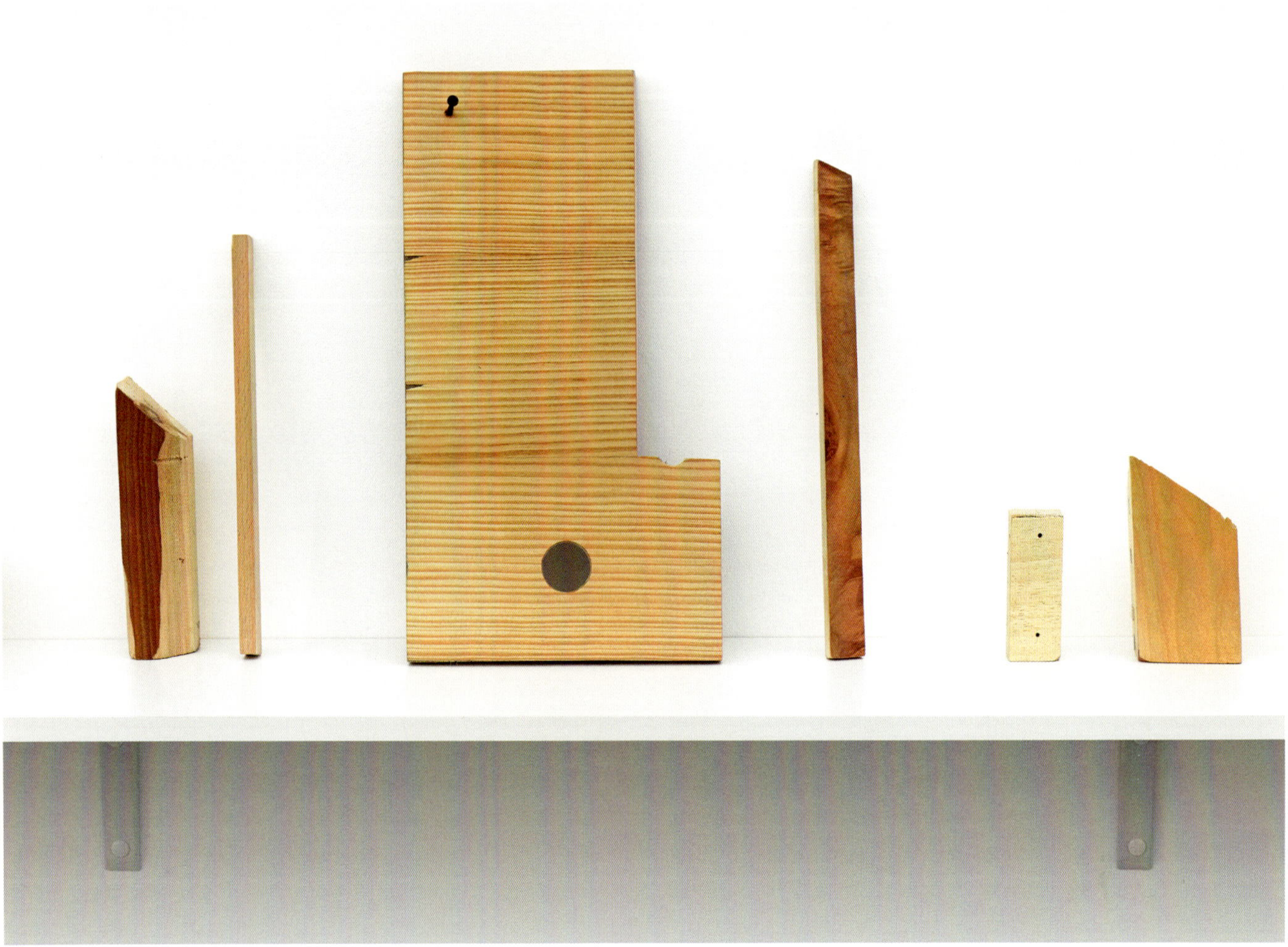

Alan Magee
Veneered Off-Cuts (detail)
2011
Wood, shelf and photographic print
48 1/16 x 108 11/16 x 9 1/16 in.
(122 x 276 x 23 cm)

previously an ad hoc tool that I had used to make another work. So at one stage the use value was one hundred per cent, and then after that particular task was completed its use value became, kind of nothing – in that sense it just became an offcut. I was also exploring the idea of the image and the object, and the value between the image and the object, and I guess the slight elements of seduction or fetishism of the image.

So they're all laminated, no? With a different type of wood?

Exactly! So this one is cluster maple, and that one… I can't recall exactly.

I'm looking at the image here and each one has a different wood veneer.

One or two of them are the same. There are 16 objects but I didn't have 16 veneers. But with some of them you can still very much see exactly what the substrate was.

Where did they come from, and this is the 'before' and this the 'after'?

It looks like that because I inverted them; I flipped them.

Oh, it's the back side.

It's the back side, exactly. I very much enjoy the idea that this is actually an image of the 'real'. It's not a time-based change, it's still existing as it is because they're flipped, then...

And then the photograph is flipped?

Exactly! So it's an image of...

Now I get it.

The 'real', and then the 'real' itself – but the veneered 'real' – so there are two layers of difference. I was also exploring the notion of veneering, the idea of covering or changing, not necessarily as a delusion, but in a sense 'believing in', and allowing yourself to go with something, maybe like Baudrillard and the simulation. I was interested in the idea of a gestural change. I knew I wanted to veneer something, but initially I was unsure of what. So the process of taking something that was kind of 'to hand' in the studio, was quite nice. It wasn't veneered for any function other than the 'act' of veneering, and there was no sense that I was trying to beautify something which required beautification, it was just the pure process of veneering an object.

How large is the piece, what's the width?

The photograph is 3 metres long.

3 metres long!

And the tallest object is 60 cm high, and there's a tiny bit of breathing

space at the top and at the bottom.
So it's quite large. So this would be about 130 – 140... 60 by 2 by 10 or something?
Around that.
Are you happy with the way you were hanging the photograph, and what is the system? It seems like it's a cable or something?
It's two high tensile cables, which is a kind of standard display unit from IKEA. I think it's actually for a shower curtain.
Was that a deliberate choice, or was it something that you had in terms of resources?
It was a mixture of both. I knew what I didn't want to do, and I felt like I didn't want to frame it.
Okay.
Because the separation would be overstating the elevation of the image, physically it was already elevated over the wood, in its display.
What about just simple pushpins or any other type of pins? Were you interested in this cable, itself?
Not necessarily; I would be flexible.
I'm just trying to understand the piece, because it seems that it's quite a strong framing device, no?
I guess it reinforces the idea of display, but again it's not necessarily the way you would display something in a gallery, it's more of a shop-window kind of display, for products. And then the shelf is another unit of display, so they're both kind of simple and understated display systems. I work with shelves quite a bit actually, as they're a way of storing; the shelf is a way of displaying but it's also a way of getting rid of something.
I'm just questioning the cables. What are the steel cables, what are they?
It's a very thin, high tensile cable.
It's not the best quality image so I can't really see it.
Yes I know, it's very hard to see – there was a restriction on file size.
I know. Okay...

Alan Magee was born in 1979 in Ireland and lives and works in London. He holds an MA in Fine Art from Central Saint Martin's College of Art and Design, London (2009). Awards include Florence Trust Studio Residency (2011); Arts Council Ireland, Travel and Training Awards and recent exhibitions include 'Endogenous', Maria Stenfors Gallery, London (2012); 'Agents of Change', Studio 1.1, London (2012) and 'Our Lives as Things', Occupy Space, Limerick, Ireland (2011).

Fay Nicolson

Sunday 17 March 2013; 17h30

Adriano Pedrosa: Before we start looking at the work I wanted to ask why you are interested in participating in 'Open Cube', and why you applied?
Fay Nicolson: Well there are a few reasons, well lots of reasons. I tend to be quite bad at applying for open submission things. That might be because I'm a little bit cynical. The thing that interested me about this was that it was obviously a private gallery that is extremely well known, that's almost like – maybe not the right analogy – but I was going to say, like the Walmart of galleries.
The Walmart!
But they have galleries everywhere and even the name 'White Cube' – it represents, it's synonymous with the modernist ideal of what a gallery is. And then I was interested in the fact that you were talking about how you were not necessarily going to disrupt that but intended to enter into that system. I've only ever seen solo shows at White Cube and I just thought that was quite an interesting thing. I was also curious about the fact that you said, or the copy on the website said, that 'this would perhaps give the opportunity for artists who might be outside of that system to enter into that system or to enter into a place that they may not otherwise have the opportunity to enter'. So I thought that was an interesting proposition. You're kind of making, or short-cutting perhaps, the unwritten rules of the way that artists might enter into that system whilst making them visible. On the other hand, it's a fantastic opportunity and I'm being completely honest here; if your work is in a gallery like this people will see it. It's an opportunity to show works in perhaps the ideal context. Also, being practical, as an emerging artist it's rare to find an opportunity to show works in a space that's going to do

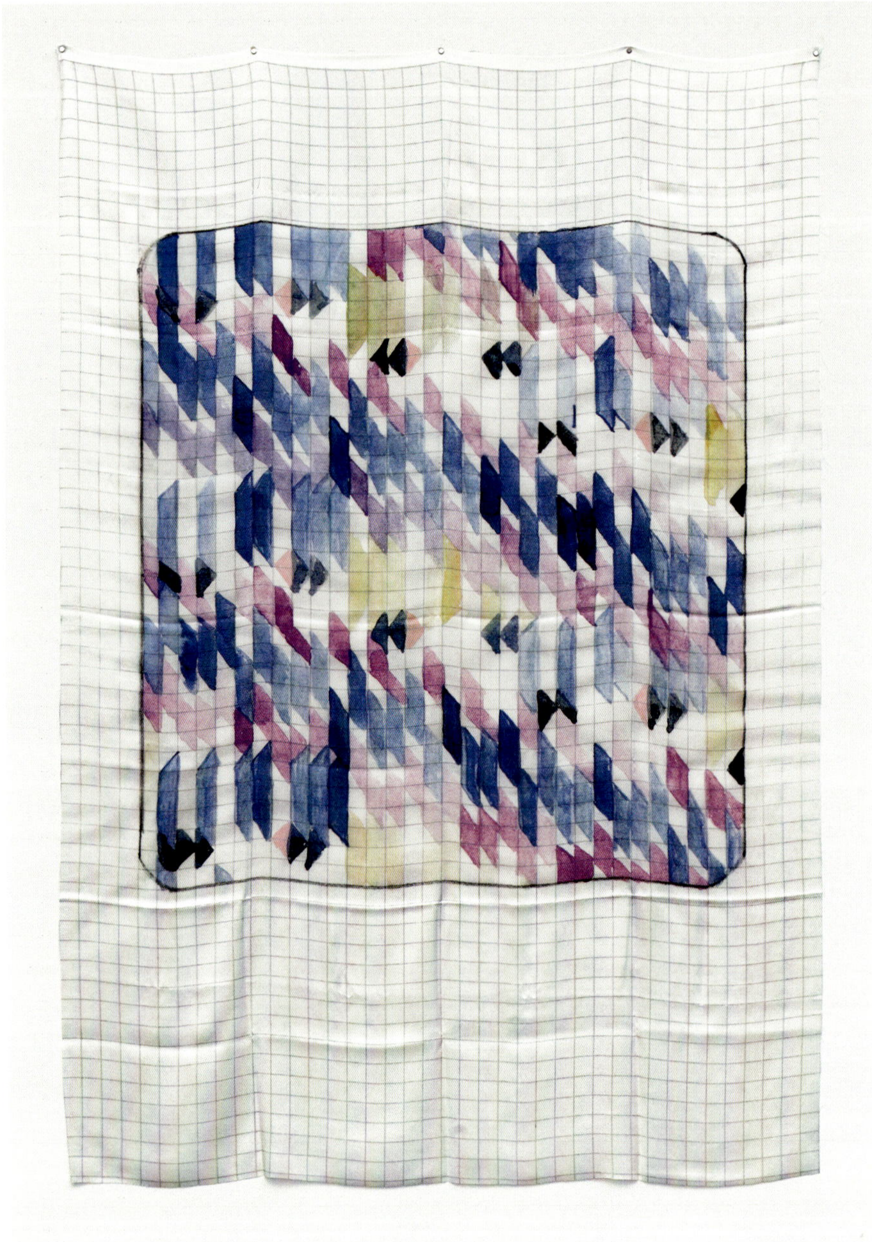

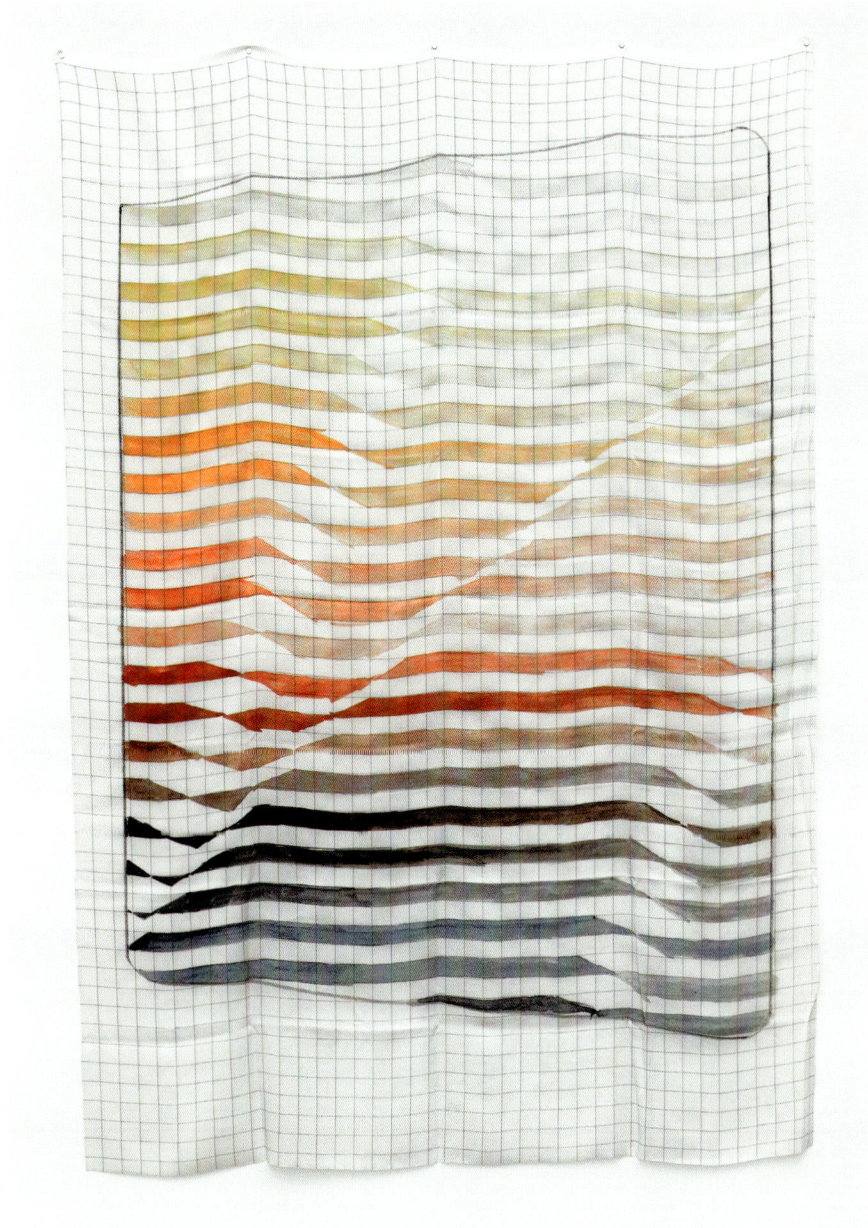

Opposite:
Fay Nicolson
We Exist! We Have the Will!
We are Producing! (blue)
2013
Digital print on silk
71 5/8 x 50 in.
(182 x 127 cm)

Right:
We Exist! We Have the Will!
We are Producing! (orange)
2013
Digital print on silk
71 5/8 x 50 in.
(182 x 127 cm)

the work justice.
They invited me to curate an exhibition and I proposed this experiment, so somehow I am trying to open up a little bit what White Cube is and what 'Open Cube' could be. That's why I'm also playing with the notion of the transparent cube which is why we are recording the conversations, and they will be published in the catalogue. That's the idea at this stage, but I will see how all this material can be put together and articulated. I know you brought some objects, some of the digital prints on silk?
I have these with me because I am in the process of making some more, but I thought it could be interesting to bring some tests.
Oh some tests, wonderful.
So this is the colour test for two of those prints.
Is this the exact same silk that you are using in the others?
Yes.
So it's always slightly shiny?
Yes, and I think I got the size wrong; they are actually bigger. They're 130 cm wide by 184 cm. Like in here all that's happened is that I've taken a snapshot of that and just dumped it on the paper, but this grid runs all the way through the whole thing. And these were some tests for some new works I'm making and here the scale is accurate.
And also the delineation of the colour is slightly irregular, or is it more precise?
It depends. I have these with me because, yet again, I was working on these and I have them at home.
They're not absolutely hard-edged?
No they're not.
So the final pieces, they also have this sort of fluid, almost watercolour like quality?
Yes. So when you're standing here there's a sharp geometrical…
But as you approach… it's really important to see them. I'm glad you arranged this. Thank you so much, because it really makes a difference when you see them in person.
And these are the new ones, but this is an example of how they start.
Oh right, that's how you do it, I see. So that's where the grid is coming from, from these drawings.
Yes, and that's why they're that size, those dimensions, they relate back to the page and maybe even as a short-circuiting between something like an instruction drawing on the one hand and on the

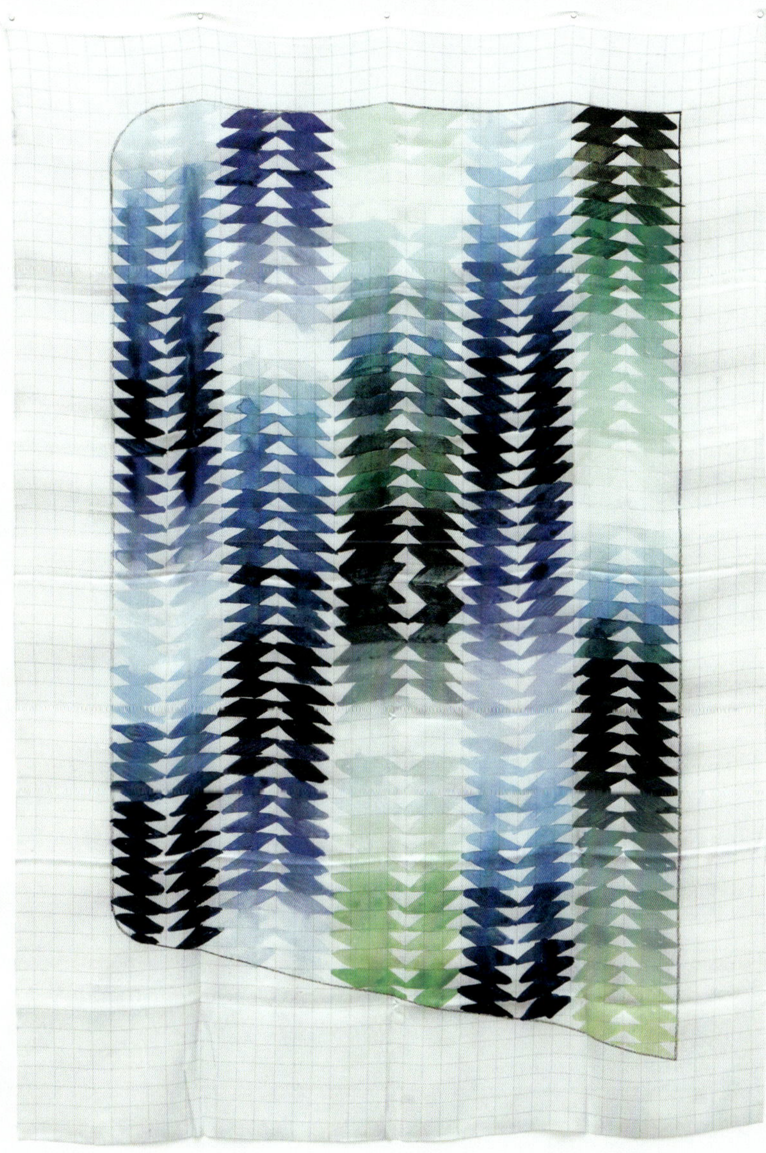

Fay Nicolson
We Exist! We Have the Will!
We are Producing! (green)
2013
Digital print on silk
71 5/8 x 50 in.
(182 x 127 cm)

other something about domestic space and modernist textile design, and Anni Albers and Gunta Stölzl. Stölzl was a Bauhaus master, kind of forced into the weaving workshop. I first started thinking about this way of working when I went to the Bauhaus archive in 2008 and saw this fantastic, very small, scrap of design for textiles, and there was something about the way they were designed with watercolours on paper that interested me. It was like this graph paper. I like the fact that it related to jacquard systems or knitting or ideas of formatting work. It's really about work and labour and this repetitive process. And then in the design there's something else that emerges that's much closer to abstract painting. I really love her work. I'm interested as well in the kind of discrepancies about how you might now relate to work like that and the way that it's been represented, and the personal narratives that come out of that. So, for example, Oskar Schlemmer's diary is quite interesting to me because it contains information that you wouldn't necessarily see in any official manifesto, document or record about the Bauhaus itself, where he might be slagging off the diet in relation to questioning his own creative powers whilst thinking about the political context. I find that kind of personal catalogue of information fascinating. Yet again I haven't read it cover-to-cover. I tend to amass material.

But are you interested in the fact that these are women of a certain period, working with textiles? Because you mentioned she was somehow forced into textiles, there is a political, feminist reading there. Is that something that interests you?

Yes, it does interest me. I wouldn't say my works are making a statement.

A statement about feminism? I agree, but they are informing the...

They revisit that moment.

Yes, especially if you are looking at art history and focusing on these artists.

Definitely. Looking back I think I was surprised by the way that things like gender relations actually impacted on something that was supposedly a kind of utopian model of education. But yes, I think that's fascinating.

And the choice of the material, silk. Why is that?

Well, I started off with the designs. In the painting process it's almost like a performance or a kind of thinking about the way that patterns

emerge and re-emerge, almost like re-visiting a kind of moment of being a textile designer, but then I've wanted to re-route or short-cut the way that they might be produced or the function of the actual design itself. So when the grid is no longer a tool for someone who is weaving, to actually decode and make the works, it becomes the surface of the aesthetic itself.
Of course.
The way I feel about them is they short-cut or re-route this in the way that they skip that physical production process and go straight from the design to something that is quite alluring or feminine.
That's what I was going to ask.
And I think in relation to some of my other works as well, they're colourful, and there are these edges that blur and you get the kind of serendipitous merging and the accident as well, when you get up quite close. But then maybe when you step back and you start to look at the way the colours... If you think of the rationale or the logic in the way that they've been constructed it's a different way of thinking, and it's almost like going back to a more mechanical way of reproducing, or maybe a cottage-industry way of working.
Yes, because it is a material for dress-making, it's coming from fine dress-making, mostly women's I would say, more than men's. I guess men can wear silk shirts but it's mostly associated with women's wear, and of course silk itself is made in a certain way that's somehow referring to this artisanal way of making.
Yes.
And over that you have the digital printing, which is somehow opposing all that
Yes, or perverting it in some way. I think that recently I've gone back to reading some of the writing of Albers and it kind of struck a chord with some of the things I've been thinking about structuring an image, and weaving as a kind of tension between a structure and a surface. And maybe other ways of mark-making, if you're thinking about how the textiles are made, where materials are gathered and kind of coalesce in a certain way.
Many filters?
Yes, and then suddenly you have the digital which kind of flattens everything down again, and you want to touch them, but can you? These are some of the things I was thinking about.
And they are not framed, you just attach them to the wall with nails?

Magnets!
Oh okay, the tiny ones.
And also when they're hanging there's something about the way they hang, they become very physical and there are slight curves and maybe illusions in the way that they hang. So for example, this bit here is actually the scan of the paper and the wrinkles in the paper, but these are the ways they hang.
And the title, We Exist! We Have the Will! We are Producing!, *is that a fragment, appropriated somehow?*
Exactly, it's from Schlemmer's diary and I took it as the title of the whole show, but then I decided that the fabric prints should be titled that way too. To be honest, it has become slightly problematic because there are three works and they all have the same title. But with that statement I really love the way it was a kind of exclamation that, 'I Will Create!', is something that might be slightly absent from teaching at college. For example my BA from St Martins – as an institution it was very much about valuing the ability to analyse the surrounding artistic context and the value of criticism. It was very much that kind of art school, well it was when I was there, whereas the RCA values material experimentation, in a way that the workshops are set up, in the way time is organised. So I think when reading Schlemmer's diaries there is something about this phrase that seemed out of time but I thought it was quite bold.
I've also been thinking about these issues. That image of Gunta Stölzl I showed you is part of a project called Weaves.
Oh really.
It tried to look at weaves as an emblem instead of grids.
Yes, fascinating.
Because the grid of course is a grid of the Modern, whereas the weave is ancient and organic and handmade, and made in an artisanal way?
Yes, and maybe also relating more to a narrative or accommodating narrative, whereas a grid is almost like... If you think back to the way it was used in an educational sense it forms a kind of table, a point.
A matrix.
Yes, that you can place disparate samples on.
Organising things and bringing them together.
Whereas with the weave, everything is connected and has implications

on the rest of the image, and if you were to pull out one thread it kinda…
Unravels in a different way.

Fay Nicolson was born in 1984 in Derby, UK and lives and works in London. She holds a BA in Fine Art from Central Saint Martin's College of Art and Design, London (2006) and an MA in Fine Art from the Royal College of Art, London (2011). Recent solo exhibitions include, 'Work with Material', Künstlerhaus Wien, Vienna (2013) and 'Bad Signs', PLAZAPLAZA, London (2012). Group exhibitions include 'A Small Hiccup', Grand Union, Birmingham (2013); 'Take Me Out', Limoncello, Art Projects, London Art Fair, London (2013) and 'Manifesta 8', Murcia, Spain (2010).

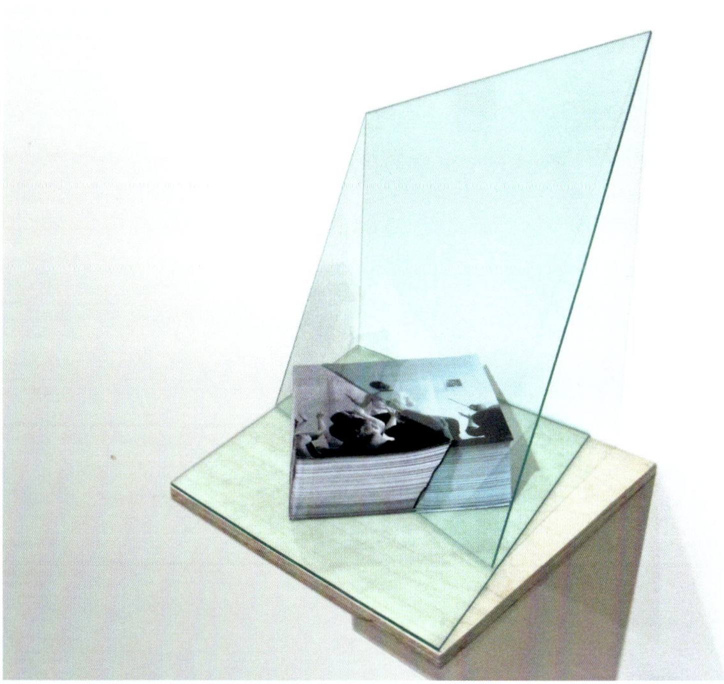

Fay Nicolson
A is for Albers
2011/2012
Sculpture with photocopies, wooden shelf and Perspex
Approx.: 11 13/16 x 15 3/4 x 19 11/16 in. (30 x 40 x 50 cm)

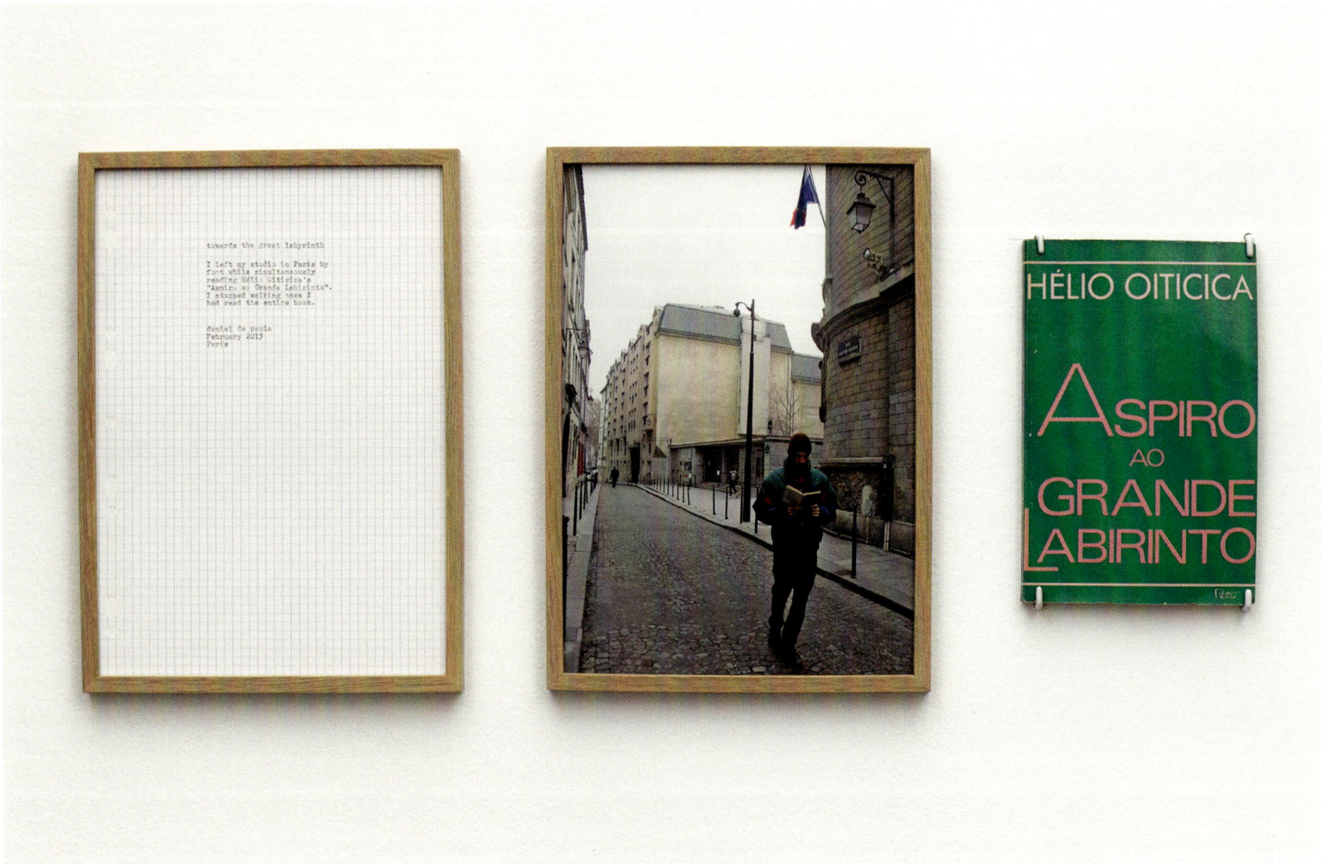

Daniel de Paula
Towards the Great Labyrinth
2013
Book, photographic
documentation and typewriter
text on squared paper
Each frame: 11 13/16 x 8 7/16 in.
(30 x 21.5 cm)
Book: 8 1/4 x 5 1/2 in.
(21 x 14 cm)

Daniel de Paula

Sunday 17 March 2013; 16h30

Adriano Pedrosa: The way that I like to begin the conversation is to ask why the artist was interested in participating in this project, why they applied, what their expectations are, and why they are interested in a show at White Cube.
Daniel de Paula: Well, I received an email from e-flux.
From Art Agenda.
As White Cube recently opened in São Paulo I thought it could have something to do with that. I read the email and was kinda surprised, as I thought it was a very sincere proposition and project because it breaks all the barriers that we usually have between galleries and artists; it's something of a more direct approach. Sometimes I'm sceptical about open calls, but this one seemed objective, and of course it's a gallery where there are a bunch of artists that I admire. I thought that, as I am already in Paris, I might as well try it out, and besides that I just thought it could be interesting to meet some other people.
What about the gallery itself, what is your perception of it?
One of the most interesting things about White Cube is that it's located in several countries in different continents, and it has this perception that it could reach art and the art world in the margins as well, and not only by being here in London. I've read and studied aspects of the white cube in college, about the structure of it and the architecture, and all the ideas about the 'white cube' and so on. I think it's something that hasn't stagnated; it just tried to do something different and go to other places. I was at the Tracey Emin show in Brazil.
And by margins you mean places like São Paulo?
Like São Paulo and Hong Kong.
I should say that this conversation is very interesting for me, in order to

understand the project I proposed, and how artists reflect on what they read. So that's why it's important to have this conversation before I look at the work.
That is something I found interesting about this gallery. Anyway, this is the 'precious' book, it's falling apart but as I've only been in Paris for a month, I wasn't able to find a nice place to print everything.
No, it's alright. And this is Towards the Great Labyrinth, *from 2013?*
This is the image and this is the text.
Did you type it?
Yes. I bought the typewriter in a flea market. I like typewriters because you have the physical reference right there. You don't have the situation of having a projection and then needing to print it out. I like the aesthetic as well, it reminds me of Conceptualism.
It does seem nostalgic in that sense, in terms of trying to mimic something from another time.
I find it easier to type on a typewriter than on a computer. I write essays.
Do you mind if I touch this?
Feel free. I think the typewriter, as well as the image not being so big, has something more intimate about to it.
And what is the idea behind the piece?
Well I've always seen Hélio Oiticica's work like a topography from a bird's eye view, which was like a city but at the same time he had this thing of drifting. So I imagined an overlapping of two different cartographies simultaneously, the book and the city, and having them interact, trying to find certain moments where the text would combine with something, with the phenomena which was happening. Of course Paris has all this historical aspect to it, which we could bring from the Situationists and from the *flâneur*, which Oiticica also did in Rio. I find it interesting to bring a private action like reading, which usually happens in a private situation, into a public space. I like this intersection and this frontier between what a person does by themselves and what they do in a public space.
You wrote: 'I left my studio in Paris by foot whilst simultaneously reading Hélio Oiticica's Aspiro ao Grande Labirinto, *and stopped walking once I had read the entire book'. How long were you on the street reading the book?*
It was about 7 hours. 7 to 8 hours.
In February 2013 in Paris! Is it important to say that it is in Paris?
I think so.

So what does Paris bring to the work?
I think it brings all this historical critique of space that Paris has had through its influential writers, like the literature of Georges Perec or the philosophy of Foucault or Deleuze. There is a spirit of Paris, a spirit of a place that activates this type of critique of space and at the same time there is a duality between the two hemispheres; this is a map from the southern hemisphere and this is from the northern hemisphere. So I'm placing both of them into the same situation, and there are some amazing texts at the end of the book where Oiticica talks about a sub-culture, the subterranean, in Brazil and South America.
I must say, I have a hard time connecting this text to Paris as it's very much from the south, from the margins. I understand the connection with the flâneur *and Perec and all that, but the fact that it's Paris…*
I needed to do this work in a city that I didn't know because of the potential to drift, and to leave your studio without having a specific direction, without being conditioned by having been there before. But for me it was also important to be in a place that was different and of another climate. All these different versions for me are important: hemisphere, climate, language…
You are going from the margin to the centre?
Yes, yes!
So you are becoming less marginal in that sense?
Could be.
Or attempting to?
Paris is a city that, at least at its centre, is so wealthy and rich and full of history and so on, yet at its *périphérique*, and the further out you go, you start seeing all the other cultures, so that at a certain point it becomes almost medieval; Paris ends and then something else starts. Interestingly, on my walk I suddenly found myself at the *périphérique* where some cops stopped me and said, 'You can't walk here', so Paris seems to illustrate a spatial equation which is bigger than itself, that is 'of the world'. I found that overlapping the two different plans and then placing it on top of the geography of Paris, was very important, especially as I was shifting them around trying to find places where they could connect.
I find it curious that it's not only a move from the margins to the centre, given that you are a Brazilian working in Portuguese, working in Paris, in France,

but also, that you are doing the work in English.
Yes but that's a... [laughing]
That's a what, tell me? Do you aspire to The Great Labyrinth*? You are using a book that is in Portuguese, the title is in Portuguese.*
There's a triangle here of languages.
That seems to be rather Eurocentric in some aspects.
I think it has to do with me, the way I was brought up you know. I speak English fluently, and sometimes even think in English, even though I've lived in Brazil, and I think this idea of the margin has shifted so much I find it hard to say that maybe...
It's still very heavy, it still exists enormously.
Yes of course.
Regardless of all the debate that's going on, and the opening up, it's still very prevalent, and particularly in Paris I would say.
One other example. For me it was important to have this flag in this picture.
What flag is it?
The European Union.
You're aspiring to The Great Labyrinth *in Paris, which I find a bit ironic. But still! [laughs]*
I even filmed the walk with a camera I attached to myself. I can show you if you like, but in the end I didn't want it to be such a performative piece and I felt the video would bring out something very performative. I find it more intimate like this, without the video, as it becomes more the documentation of a process and of an action.
What about this piece here?
apparition.
It's originally in English?
No, originally in Portuguese, *aparição.*
apparition*, which is?*
Which was at the Centro Cultural São Paulo. I was selected from an open call and it was my intention to work with public property as it was a museum. I wanted to do something that had a relationship with the architecture, so I went to the Department of Lighting in the city of São Paulo and asked them if I could get a lamppost to use for the exhibition. It's a piece I like a lot.
It was borrowed?

Yes. I had two options. One was a loan request and the other was a donation request. I received the loan request because they didn't want to give me the donation request, and once it was installed it won the Acquisition Prize.
Of the Centro Cultural São Paulo?
Yes, so they had to change the loan into a donation and it was interesting because it just shifted from one public space to another public space, one public institution to another public institution.
It also belongs to the city as they are both the Municipality of São Paulo.
Exactly, and I got paid for that because I won the prize. After this work the Centro Cultural made another five lampposts which were donated and installed in the surrounding area, because they didn't have money to buy lampposts and, given that a guy was murdered four years ago in a very dark alley nearby, I saw it as an interesting manoeuvre – this whole strategy of working with public institutions from the same city. The lamppost I used had a photo-sensitive cell installed in it, which was powered from an electric source outside of the museum, so it lights up whenever it gets dark and, because of the bureaucracy and all these problems we have they didn't communicate that information to the Centro Cultural São Paulo. As you can see there's a window through which you could see the lamppost at night from the avenue below, so when the entire museum's lights were off you still had this lamppost on, projecting light outside the museum. It was important that the piece was visible through the window, where you could see...
The lamppost in real life?
The lamppost from the outside.
Yes, but this is very specific to Centro Cultural São Paulo or...
Not to Centro Cultural São Paulo but it works in...
In a space where you have the same. The lamppost you use for the work inside the gallery needs to be the same as those that are outside, and you need to be able to view those lampposts from within the gallery.
Yes, of course. You need a window, something that's glass and so on.
So we couldn't do it here for example because you can't see anything of the outside; White Cube is really enclosed.
Isn't there glass?
A nice glass cube, no, [laughs loudly] but there is a window that's coated in white laminate. I'm just trying to think of different possibilities because I thought it

would be quite an interesting piece to replicate. I'm exploring different options, but it could be interesting to see how this would translate into the London context, in White Cube. Particularly because I think White Cube, more so than Centro Cultural São Paulo, has this heavy layer of institutionalisation and objectification and commodification. It's not 'transparent' architecture, such as this one, and this place doesn't really look so much like a traditional gallery.

Daniel de Paula was born in 1987 in Boston, USA and lives and works between Itapevi, São Paulo and Paris. He holds a BA in Art from Fundação Armando Alvares Penteado, São Paulo (2012). Recent exhibitions and residencies include 'Espaços Independentes – a alma é o segredo do negócio', Galerias Funarte de Artes Visuais, São Paulo (2013); Cité Internationale des Arts Residency, Paris (2013); 'Da próxima vez eu fazia tudo diferente', Pivô, São Paulo (2012); 'Programa de Exposições', Centro Cultural São Paulo, São Paulo (2011) and 'Prêmio EDP nas Artes', Instituto Tomie Ohtake, São Paulo (2010).

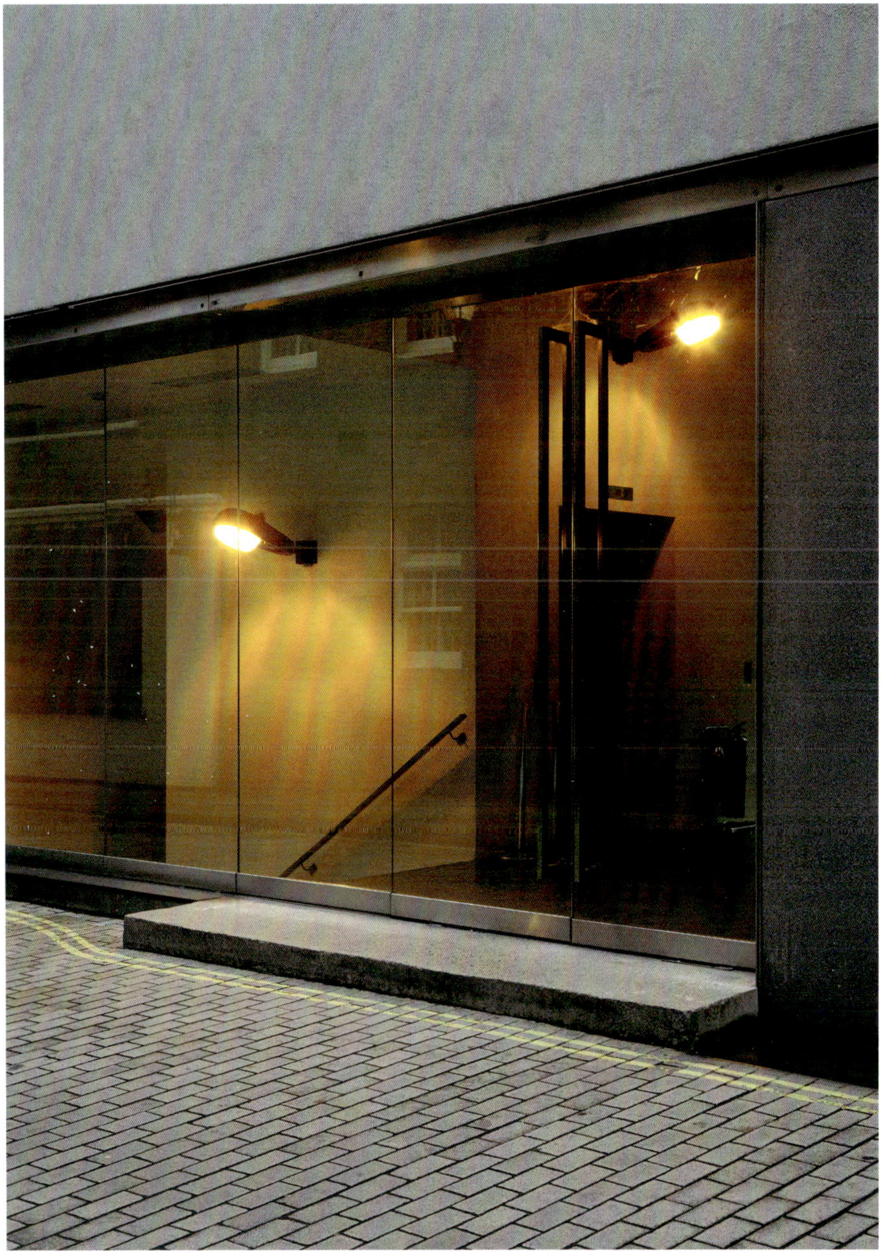

Daniel de Paula
ascension
2013
Two public street lights borrowed from the Lighting and Transportation Commissioning Department of Westminster City Council, photo-sensitive cells, wire and independent electrical circuit
Dimensions variable

Kritische
Miethajen!
Statt

Nada Prlja

Saturday 16 March 2013; 12h30

Adriano Pedrosa: Why have you applied to 'Open Cube' and why are you interested in participating in this project?
Nada Prlja: It was mainly the brief that I liked, where you wrote about your intentions, like bringing in people who are not very established in the private gallery world. I was also curious about how a work belonging to the public sphere could be translated into the gallery space – how you do this and why? I was curious to experiment with those things.
And the work in particular is Peace Wall*?*
Yes.
A work you made for the 2012 Berlin Biennial?
Yes, they commissioned it and organised everything. It was very much public art, and quite a big wall that blocked Friedrichstrasse, one of the longest streets in Berlin and really well known, with posh, beautiful stores on one side. I wanted to be on Friedrichstrasse because it drastically changes from a really wealthy street into quite a poor one. It's one of the areas that has the largest number of migrants and unemployed people.
So from the very gentrified to the workers or the jobless.
Previously it was 5 minutes from Checkpoint Charlie and before it was gentrified it was the poor area of West Berlin, because no one wanted to live close to the wall then, only migrants and the poor moved in.
Is it a pre-existing structure?
Everything was constructed just for this piece. The work was made of big concrete blocks, which supported the two side panels – one side was

Nada Prlja
Peace Wall (detail)
2013
MDF panels, paint, fabric and paper
172 1/16 x 446 7/8 x 1/2 in.
(437 x 1135 x 1.2 cm)

MDF and the other was metal.

So you could really see it was just a staged situation. How did you get the authorisation to do it, and was it a pedestrian street?

Being one of the biggest streets it's mostly for cars, but people can pass. We blocked the street.

The city allowed that?

We negotiated for one year.

How long did you block the street for?

It was a little bit less than two months; I think 53 days or something.

It's amazing that the city allowed it.

But that was only at the last moment. Initially we did get a 'Yes', but they changed their minds because other streets were blocked, and then said we were completely blocking all the traffic. In Berlin they have a particular situation in their need to be open to culture, so we said to them, 'Well, you have all these other things that are blocking streets to improve them, but this is a work of art, so you cannot ignore this in relation to the others; you allowed the other ones and now you cannot stop this'.

Because it's a work of art?

Then two weeks before the opening they said 'Yes!' which we were really surprised by.

And you managed to complete it all in two weeks?

First was the biennial opening and my work was billed for five days later as we didn't want everything to happen on the same day. We thought it's just going to become an attraction for art tourism, so we left it till later and said it could be something for the community to relate to, and somehow they have their own impression of it. It took three days to put it up, so it was quite fast.

How did the community react to having this piece and it blocking their way?

For most of them it was really different, and this is the first work of mine where I've had so many positive and negative comments. They were annoyed that we stopped the traffic – this was the biggest issue all the way through the project – even after I explained that I wanted to relay the idea that there are still walls in modern cities, and that we have to address this and the gentrification of this poor area; they are going to invest around 26 million Euros to develop and change the area. Despite wanting to trigger big topics with a work of art they said, 'No, we cannot

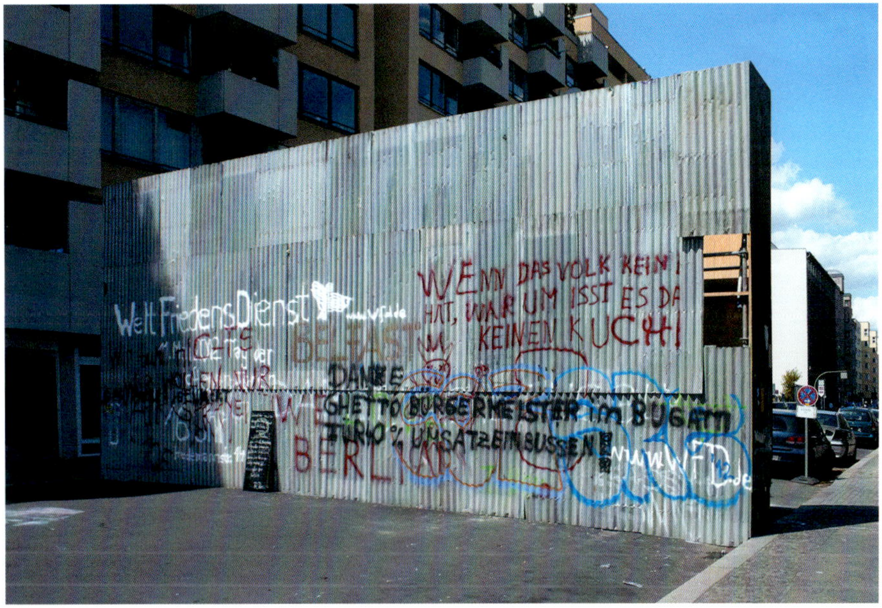

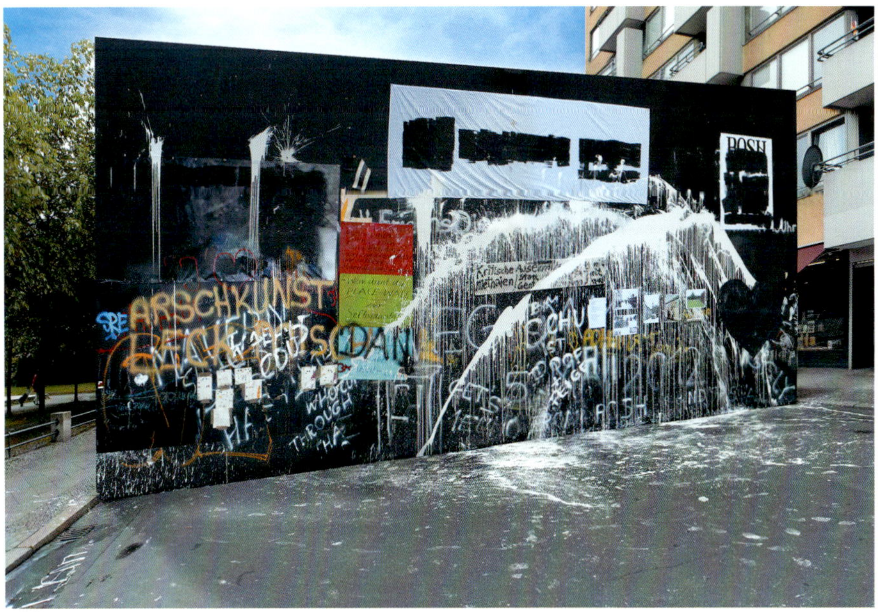

Nada Prlja
Peace Wall
Installation views in Friedrichstrasse, Berlin, 2012

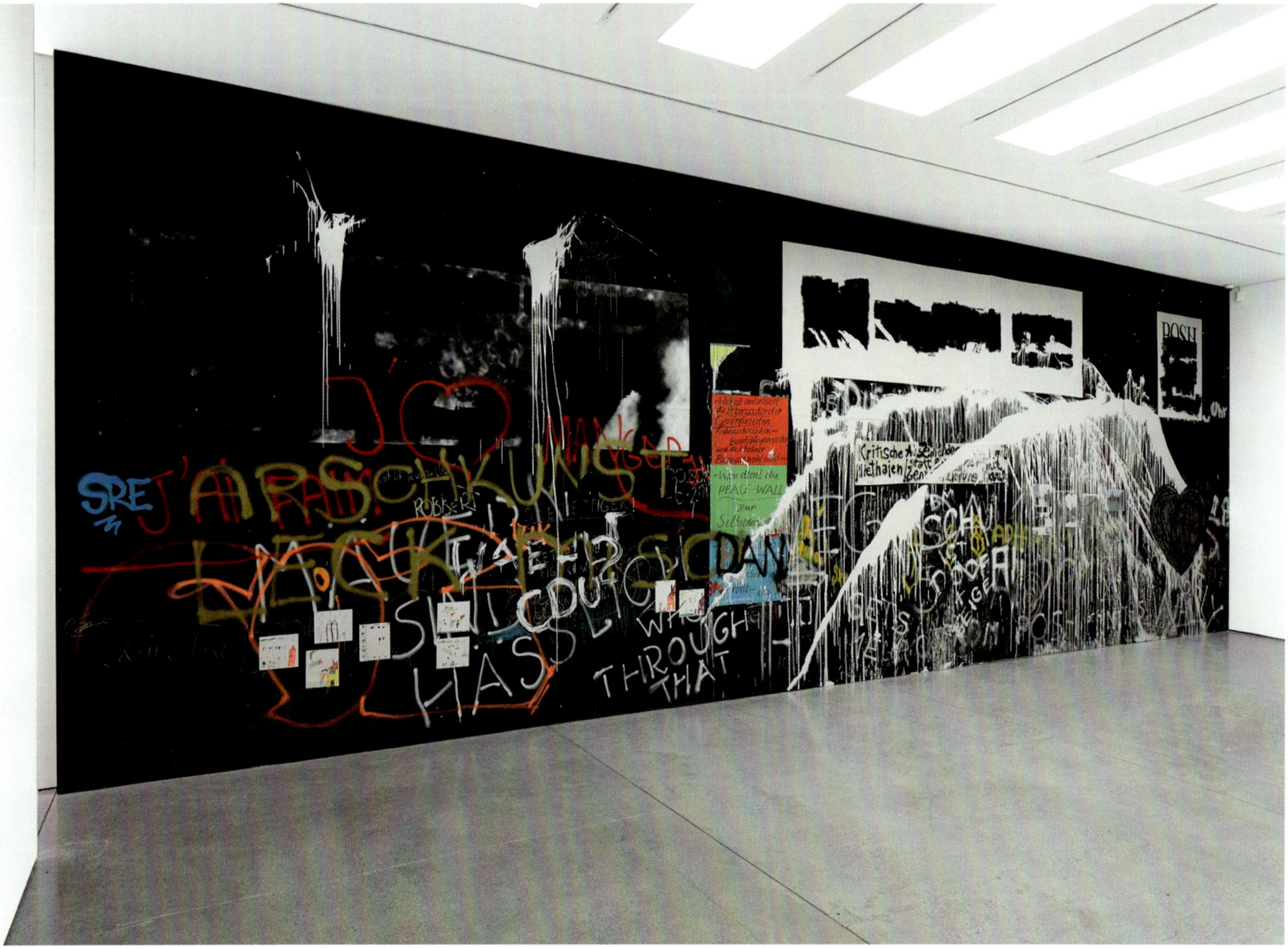

Nada Prlja
Peace Wall
2013
MDF panels, paint,
fabric and paper
172 1/16 x 446 7/8 x 1/2 in.
(437 x 1135 x 1.2 cm)

pass with the car!', and it's like, 'Oh, but now you have a medium to talk about your position. Being poor and unemployed is a bigger issue, so you can address these issues now; you have this wall and you have so much media attention'. Some of them used it, but the strongest negative side against the wall were the local shops. For me this was unusual and I was intrigued by it because for them it was unacceptable to be seen on the other side, on the 'bad' side as they called it. They wanted the gentrification to bring better clients into their stores and so on; by better they mean richer. I also had positive responses as some people wanted to talk about the gentrification, and the groups that wanted a slice of the 26 million Euro cake to build their own centres etc. – which in Berlin is not really monitored. There are so many things you can do if you are an investor and have money; you can do whatever. So for them it was a good message but for others not. It was really very mixed.

After two or three weeks I was in London, but later on there were all these happenings and politics started getting involved, with one political party supporting it, and the other one against it. So for the last two weeks I returned to Berlin, and treated it very much like I was 'present', as it's a work that I can talk to people about, see how they react and see what we can do. In those last two weeks I spent a lot of time talking to people and then we decided maybe 10 days before the end, to take it down. The people felt that the message was clear, and that we had said what we wanted to say. They really felt uncomfortable about the blockage so they asked us to take it down, which for me was a very difficult decision, but at the same time I said, 'We can do it because I think it's important for art and culture to show its soft spot. If someone is saying something you can have the openness to accommodate that'. I think if it was a political gesture they would find a way not to accept what other people say. So I said, 'Okay, I will really consider what they are saying', and I had also become concerned as it had become too much of a local political game between those supporting it, and those not supporting it. I just thought that I should not be manipulated by these different political influences over the work, so we decided to take it down early as a symbolic gesture, and to bring it indoors – not only into a gallery space but a commercial gallery space.

Did it seem to neutralise a lot of these references, museologise or even gentrify or commercialise them?

Of course it has that aspect and as artists I think we like playing with those things, so I said, 'Okay, what will I do as an artist, what can I do with this work?' It was in a place where it was very important, with all those things happening in the community, in the media and around it – even people involved in culture reacted to it differently – so I said, 'Okay, I have this work which is completely recycled, is completely ruined, it doesn't exist as the actual work because I insisted that I really didn't want this to become a work of art; I could have put it wherever I wanted to. The question now was how we as artists look at the things around us, or how we deal with our work? This moment of re-creating the same work has a new beginning or a new question. So how do you take a work that was so important and working so intensely…

So many struggles and discussions on different levels. In the political, with the community and with circulation, all this in one of the most loaded political exhibitions in recent past – the '7th Berlin Biennale', in 2012 – which was very much against the market and art-as-commodity.

I always imagined doing an exhibition with art that somehow represents these conflicting situations. For example, after the war, you have a lot of artists who were in the army, like the Nazis, and what they did was they painted all these crashes, and planes in water, and all the remains of the actual happenings. You have the same thing in Ireland and this is all in the 20th Century, so you have artists recording this, like the burning of the houses, just to document something that was happening, and I think this process for me would somehow be the same – how can you now, as an artist, document something that was very important, and in recording it, does it somehow lose something? Does how you work as an artist add extra value, and what is the actual difference between working in the public sphere and working in a protected gallery space where everybody when entering goes, 'Oh okay, this is a work of art'.

Because it was not made to look pristine or beautiful, people wondered, 'Oh is this art, or is it not, or what is it trying to say?' Of course through this reproduction or replica of the original, you pose the question, 'Can this still be questionable in terms of the political and social aspect or does it ask other questions?' Does it question what we do as artists, how we create our work and how it works when it's within the gallery space?

Yes, definitely, especially a project titled 'Open Cube' in a space called White Cube.

How would you bring this into the gallery, because a reconstruction of the full piece with its metal structure is of course impossible?
Now what we're looking at is this image of the wall, at the black side of the wall, probably the one which was more affected by graffiti and people's actions upon it.
Was the graffiti done by you?
All the graffiti was done by other people. I never touched anything.
You just left it black?
Yes, once it was built, it was painted black.
And how would you reproduce that, how would you bring this into White Cube?
For me this belongs to them, and somehow I almost feel like I would be exploiting them if I just took it as it is physically. As I said, it was all destroyed, so the only way to represent this is to replicate it, which would mean becoming an artist again and repainting it in the closest way possible to the original. First it was the charcoal, then the rain, and then it was painted black, so going step-by-step, and basically re-creating...
The writing on the wall.
Yes.
Directly on the gallery wall?
Directly onto panels I think.

Nada Prlja was born in Sarajevo, Bosnia and Herzegovina and lives and works in London. She holds a degree from the Academy of Fine Arts, Skopje, Macedonia (1997) and an MPhil Research degree from the Royal College of Art, London (2003). Recent exhibitions include '7th Berlin Biennale', Berlin (2012); 'Manifesta 8', Murcia, Spain (2010) and 'International Biennial of Graphic Arts', Ljubljana (2009). Public presentations include Nottingham Contemporary (2013); ICA, London (2011) and Tate Britain (2009).

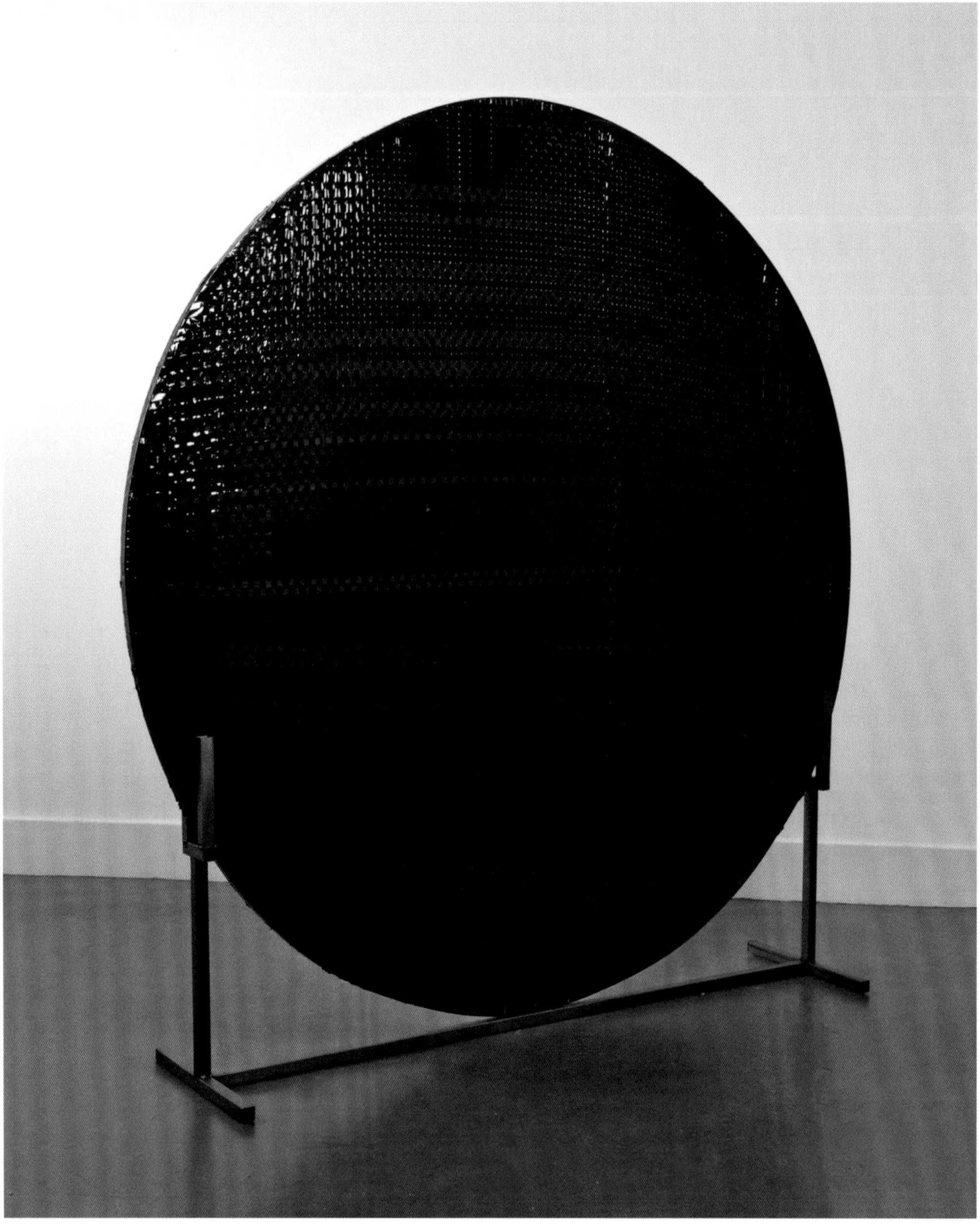

Nicky Teegan

Saturday 16 March 2013; 18h00

Adriano Pedrosa: Why were you interested in participating in the project?
Nicky Teegan: I just thought it was a really good opportunity for emerging artists to be able to access such a public platform.
What about the gallery itself. Was there anything about the gallery that interested you?
Well, White Cube as an institution is kind of global and it has a really good programme of events and exhibitions, so it's kind of part of the core. White Cube and the Tate, and the Barbican are the first point of contact for contemporary art in London.
And you are based here in London?
Yes.
So do you also think about the type of work that is exhibited here, do you relate to the work? Do you follow the programme and see the exhibitions?
Yes, I come and see the exhibitions, mostly in Bermondsey because just the size of the space is really exciting and it's a good opportunity to see international artists on your doorstep.
So I have some of your images here. Tell me more about The Void.
Well this specific piece is part of a body of objects. It's made from woven VHS tape and all the VHS tapes are Science Fiction movies like *Logan's Run* and *Planet of the Apes*, mostly 1970s Science Fiction. I guess it's just an object, yet it performs quite a theatrical function. I'd rather call it an object, than a sculpture. A lot of the work that I make deals with subverting everyday objects, specifically outmoded technologies, into objects of fetish, devotional objects or part of a collection, something that you worship, or something that becomes part of a ritual. So this is an object which would be the centrepiece for a ritual. Circles interest me

Nicky Teegan
Void
2012
Woven VHS tape over
a bent steel ring
Ø 72 1/16 in. (Ø 183 cm)

because they are mystical forms, sites of incantation. This object is used in different scenarios. Sometimes it works as an autonomous object, then other times it's an object that features in a film or an object that features in an installation, or alongside another film, so it acts as a presence and serves many functions within the work. *Prayer Battery* deals with this same idea of fetishizing and subverting objects into devotional objects and ritual. The audio piece is playing off an endless loop cassette, with these sounds that I make with these instruments and my voice. The sound pieces often set up the atmosphere for the installations, or present a narrative for whatever ritual or anything that's going on. This produced a kind of drone that set the atmosphere for the exhibition space. The endless loop cassette plays until it destroys itself, so the original recording no longer exists.

It's just a few minutes?

It's 6 minutes.

They were for answering machines, is that it?

All of the audio pieces I make are analogue. I like using low-fi technologies because of its handmade DIY tactility, and the fact that they almost act in an autonomous way by degrading. This piece played until it sounded like white noise.

And how long did that take?

It took about 5 days.

And what was the sound like right at the beginning?

It's essentially quite droney. It already has a white noise feeling about it, but different. I use handmade mics to record the sound, so it's very, very low-fi, and there's quite an ascension with the sound which will get louder.

Okay.

The sound is what you can hear from these speakers. The object in the background that is a battery, is a sculpture I made that generates this charge of the sound in the room. I'm quite interested in how people put these power placements onto objects. I recently came across a UFO group in London called The Aetherius Society who use an object called a 'Prayer Battery'. They believe that if they chant into that object it will store positive energy, and whenever a catastrophe happens in the world, they will be able to release this positive energy, curing everything. I'm interested in different belief systems like that so I made this object,

which is supposed to store all this energy in the room; for generating collective thought.
What are those cables for?
Whilst the cassette tape is playing contact mics are attached to the object that is playing, forming two sounds. There is a noise from the object, which is just white noise, and then a drone in the background.
So this work also plays the endless cassette?
Yes.
It plays here, and then it also captures...
The sound from the object. It's quite a loud vibrating type of sound.
But the object here, the sound that's captured, is also heard somewhere?
Yes, out of these speakers.
Again?
Yes.
So it blends?
They play at the same time.

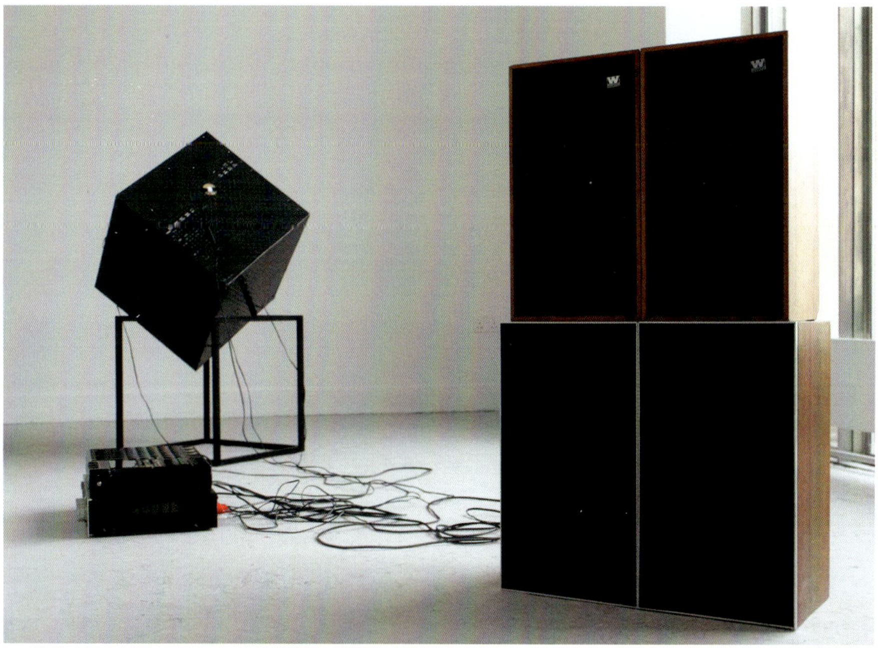

Nicky Teegan
Prayer Battery
2012
Woven VHS tape, steel, contact microphones, tascam 4 track, integrated amplifier, 4 leak speakers, audio piece on endless loop cassette
Dimensions variable, sculpture: 59 1/16 x 59 1/16 in. (150 x 150 cm)

And the Prayer Battery?
It is made from steel cubes of equal dimension, one of which is woven and the other not.
Considering your use of the cubes and the disk, squares and circles – do you have an interest in geometric abstraction?
I specifically like working with circles, and cubes are a new thing for me.
It's like the concepts of empty and full, and it almost seems like you are trying to explain that.
The relationship to working with the cube is partially just me being interested in the shape of the cube used in museum practices, and its use in the presentation of objects like the plinth, or the Sony Cube. I also like the formalism of cubes and with circles it's more of an interest in this idea of something being full and simultaneously empty, and the kind of paradox that exists between the two of them, which is why the circle is quite prevalent in my work. With cubes it's essentially a formalist interest and the hard lines are something that interests me too.
And abstraction as well then?
I guess there's an abstraction. They're quite new to my practice.
Thinking about mid-century, geometric abstraction in a very contaminated way. It's not the pure, detached, ideal geometric abstraction of the high modernist grid, because the analog element brings in the 'white noise', it completely consumes it, as if geometric abstraction was becoming a ruin. Does that make sense to you?
Kind of.
When the 'white noise' consumes geometric abstraction completely, you're erasing it too, and depleting it completely. You can think of a parallel in terms of high modernism, and the utopian ideals of mid-century geometric abstraction.
I guess so. This process of negating itself.
As if the course of history and time would consume it completely. If you're playing and playing and playing it, it eventually becomes a ruin.
At the same time it's erasing itself and repeating itself so it becomes this kind of loop, essentially negating itself.
It does eat itself up completely, no?
Yes, it does.
It doesn't repeat itself perfectly every time; it's not digital. For how many days did it play?
Around 5 days.
If it just continued to play would there be a specific moment when the sound

changed, or would there be a moment when it just stopped changing and got to a certain...?
It gets to a certain point where it essentially becomes white noise.
Like on the third day, fourth day or something?
It started to warp and stretch.
And at some point it just breaks I'm sure.
Well, now it's just become white noise.
Do you think that at some point it will just break?
Well of course it will break.
And then the process stops, and then history stops somehow, and that's the end of history.
Yes.
Have you ever thought about that in terms of high modernism?
No, I've never thought about it in terms of high modernism.
I am thinking about geometric abstraction in terms of high modernism.
Okay.
And what does geometric abstraction represent? It represents this utopian ideal where things are perfect, a grid for modern living. Consider the International Style in modernist architecture, everything was orthogonal, a perfect grid, and you have to live in a utopian world, but after all these years we realised it was not quite like that. That's what I'm talking about, the ruins somehow, of this modernist ideal. Does that make sense?
It's making sense, it's become quite dystopian through that quest.
It's the failed ideas of high modernism in architecture and in life itself. It was a model for life. If you look at several different iterations of geometric abstraction, Concretism and Constructivism, there were some different ones but there was this idea that this would be the high point of modernism in the visual arts, no?
Sure.

Nicky Teegan was born in 1987 in Ireland and lives and works in London. She holds a BA in Visual Arts Practice from Dun Laoghaire Institute of Art, Design and Technology, Dublin (2009), and an MA in Fine Art from Chelsea College of Art and Design, London (2012). She is a founding member of Ormond Studios, Dublin. Recent exhibitions include 'MA Fine Art Show 2012', Chelsea College of Art and Design, London (2012); 'SWITCH/OVER', Wimbledon Space, Wimbledon College of Art, London (2012) and 'Invite or Reject', Chicago Loop Alliance, Chicago (2011).

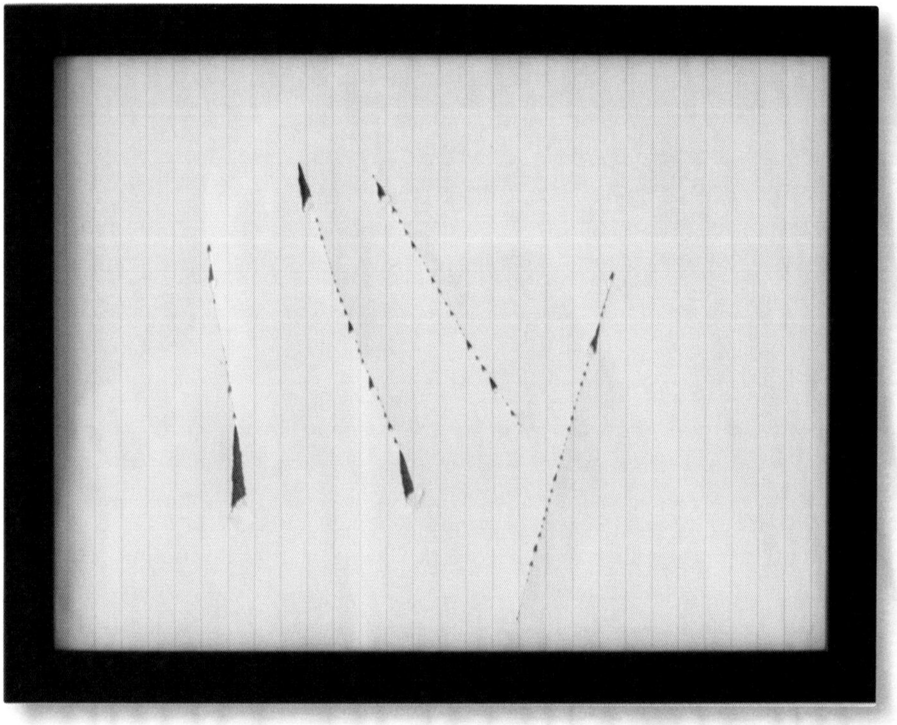

Jacopo Trabona
Untitled
2011
Diamond on paper
10 3/8 x 7 15/16 in.
(26.3 x 20.1 cm)

Jacopo Trabona

Saturday 16 March 2013; 12h00

Adriano Pedrosa: I wanted to ask you why you were interested in this project; why did you apply?
Jacopo Trabona: Because it's a great opportunity to exhibit in a gallery like this with a curator and because, to be honest, my work is at a stage in which it deserves a context, a nicer context to be shown in.
A nicer context?
It's sad, but in a way it attracts me. Talking about the gallery context I think, can likewise be related to this work. You can add something, you can add value by showing it in a high context, in a proper 'Fine Art' context. That may be sad, but I'm attracted to that.
Sad?
Sad that as an artist I'm attracted to this addition of value, yet I find it interesting.
Addition of value to the work?
To the practice and to the work as well. I think that if this object is sold it could be part of the concept of the work, and it raises some questions. A work like that in a way deals with economy, with currency and with circulation, so the fact itself of selling it, as exchange value, is something that could be pretty interesting.
So what about in terms of the career?
Of course I think it could be a really important stage in my career. I'd be lying otherwise.
What about Untitled*?*
This is a sheet of paper I carved using a diamond. I was interested in the fracture between the fragile medium, which is paper, and the diamond – the preciousness of the diamond which is not exhibited. Just this *idea* of

the diamond, as you can get it from the caption – the material is 'Diamond on paper'.
And it's one, two, three, four scratches?
Four scratches.
On lined paper?
Yes.
How large is this piece, A4?
Yes, A4 actually.
And are we sure it's really a diamond?
Yes!
Or are we not really sure?
No, no. I'm sure.
You really did it with a diamond?
Yes, I really did it with a diamond. My uncle used to have this diamond and I stuck it on a pen by just using tape, and I just carved it like that, like with a pen. In a way I drew something! I've entered a contest with this piece.
A contest?
Yes, I submitted the work into the drawing section because it was divided according to mediums, which was kind of stupid.
Where was that?
In Florence.
Okay, and you submitted that work?
As a drawing. Of course that kind of exhibition wasn't really advancing contemporary art because of the very fact of separating mediums. I don't think it matters anymore; to have a drawing section, an installation section, a sculpture section.
Is there a comment somehow on diamonds – on this very precious material? Perhaps there's a comment or some connection to be made between art and luxury goods?
Of course.
Useless, but very precious.
You can read it that way, but I didn't think about any precise political aims. I don't want to be obvious. You can think about that or you can get it in an indirect, oblique way.
Indirect, okay.
Yes.

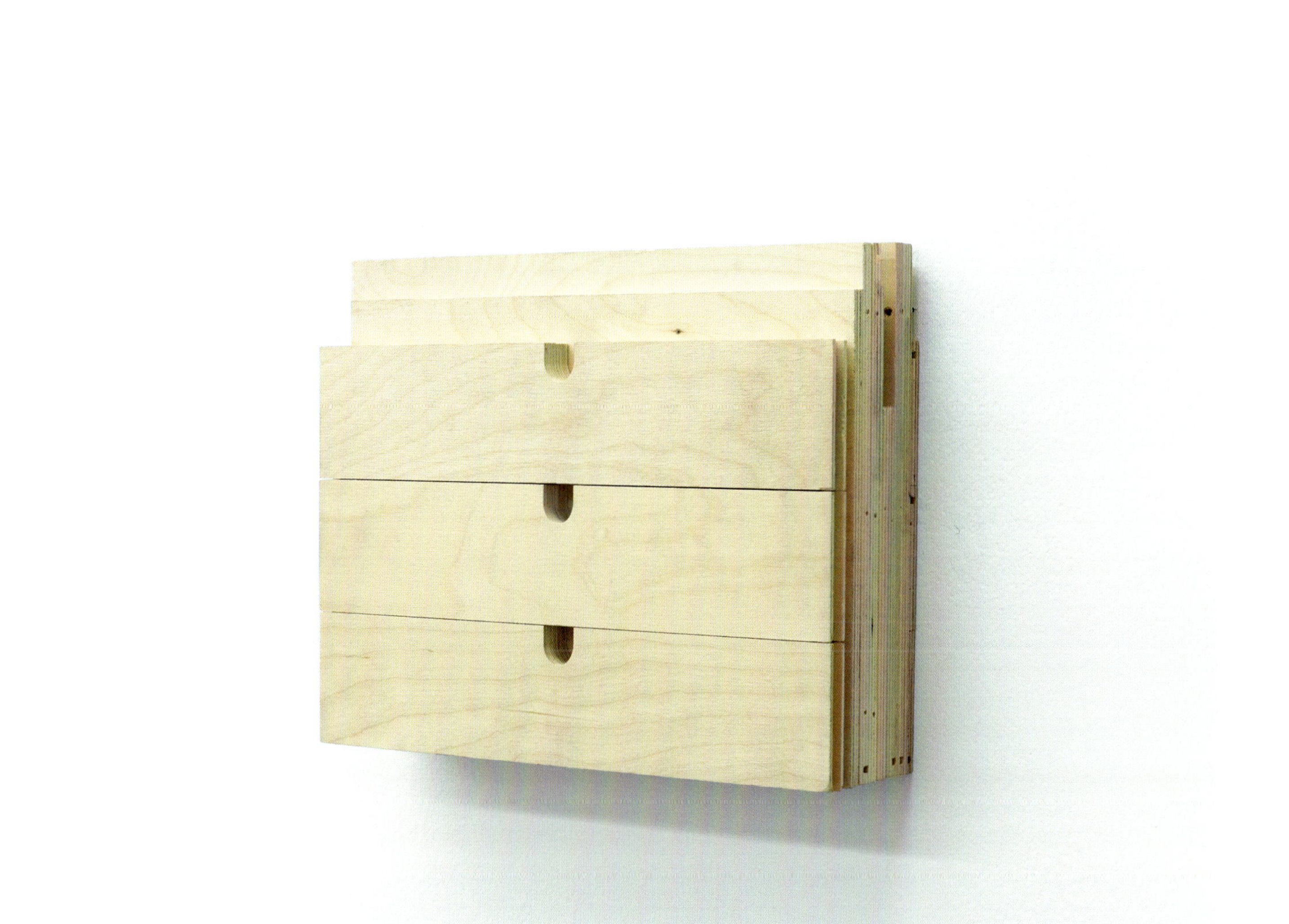

Jacopo Trabona
Bas-Relief
2010
Glue on wood
13 9/16 x 10 1/4 in.
(34.5 x 26 cm)

And also it's just the idea of adding value?
Yes.
The paper was in contact at some point with this very precious material, but that's the history. The technique tells the history of it, as if this very plain paper could now acquire a value such as that of diamonds?
Yes, my idea is utopian in a way.
But also perverse?
Yes.
Did you think of Lucio Fontana?
I've looked at Fontana's canvases. When I decided to make it, in a formal way I was copying from Fontana's canvases.
And the paper. Why did you choose a lined paper as opposed to a blank one?
I guess it was a formal matter, because this combination of the oblique line and the pattern of the vertical line was interesting. It's not part of the concept itself I would say.
It seems that you're trying to use this very common type of paper, and the lines of that piece of paper are somehow proof of the common origins of that paper, as opposed to a fine art paper?
It's supposed to be a sketch-book paper – you can write on it.
That's what I'm saying 'as opposed to a fine art paper'.
Yes, exactly.

Jacopo Trabona was born in 1989 in Italy and lives and works in London. He graduates in 2013 with an MA from Chelsea College of Art and Design, London. Recent exhibitions include 'RIVAlutAction', Riva Lofts, Florence (2012); 'B x H x Me', A + A Gallery, Venice (2012); '95th Collective Young Artists', Bevilacqua La Masa Foundation, Venice (2011) and 'Basi Prize', Cava Roselle, Grosseto, Italy (2011).

Caitlin Yardley

Saturday 16 March 2013; 17h30

Adriano Pedrosa: I wanted to ask you why you were interested in participating in this project, what drew you to apply and what your expectations are?
Caitlin Yardley: There wasn't a lot of information about the project and I didn't get to research it for very long before I found that the application was due, but from what I could see I had kind of established that you were looking to work within, but against, the gallery setting. I've worked with commercial galleries and I've worked with public galleries and whenever I've worked with a commercial gallery it's always been as semi-independent.
So what about this gallery?
The gallery itself reflects the kind of context that I would one day like to be seen in I suppose. I'm not in any way saying that I'm at that level right now, but there are a number of galleries in London that I do follow and this is one that I have followed for years.
The idea of the project is also to undo the sort of expectations one would have in terms of high gallery practices, with blue-chip type artists. When they asked me to do a show I proposed this and it was a bit of a negotiation, but finally it was agreed that I could do this democratic open call. This is why we are recording the interviews, in order to include them in the catalogue, in the name of transparency. Out of all the applications that came through the system, I only chose to interview artists that I had never heard of, so that was another interesting element for me, trying to use this platform in a different way somehow. Having said that, I also wanted to ask you about this particular piece that we're looking at, Peripheral Orbit (b) *from 2012.*
Yes.
Where was this exhibited?

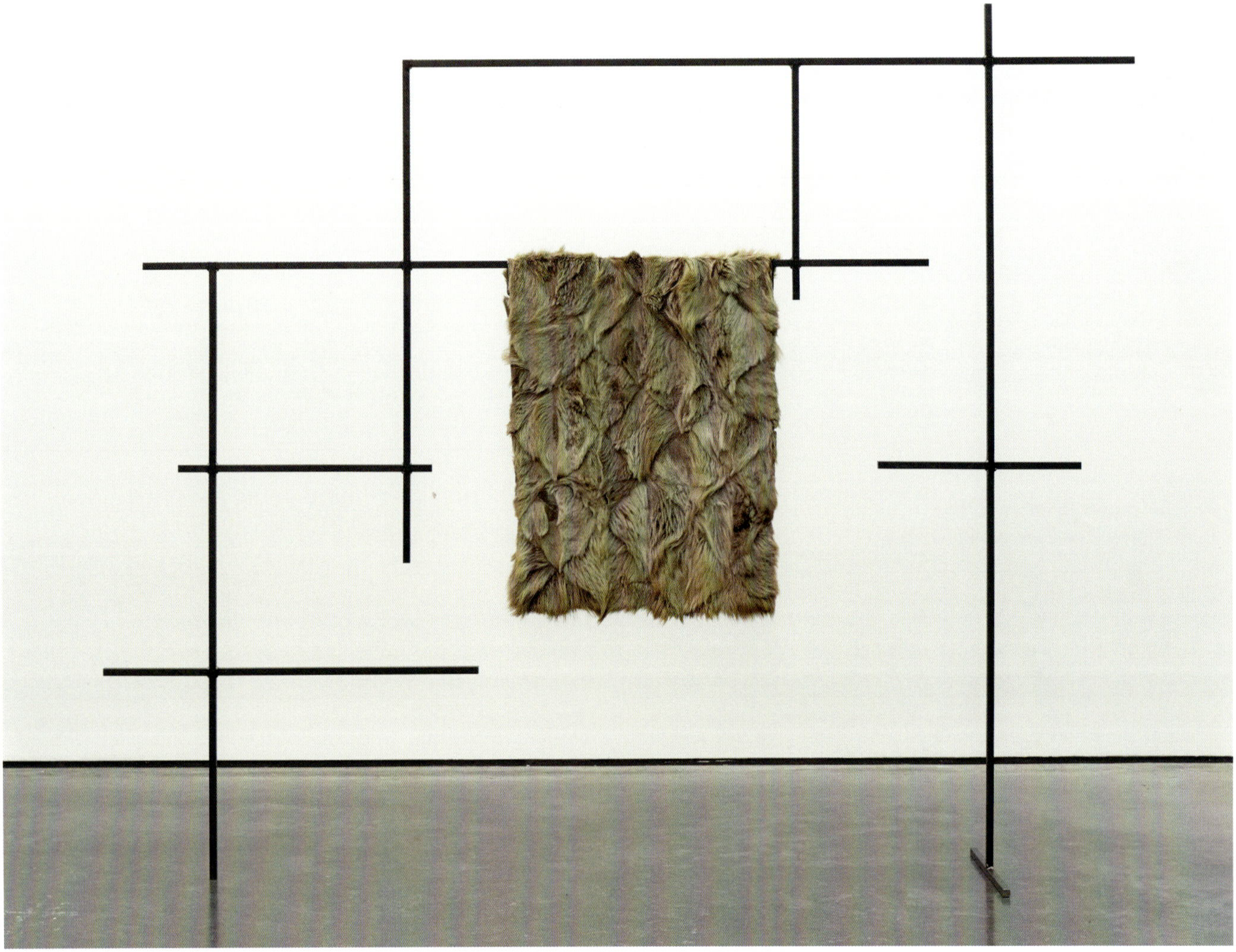

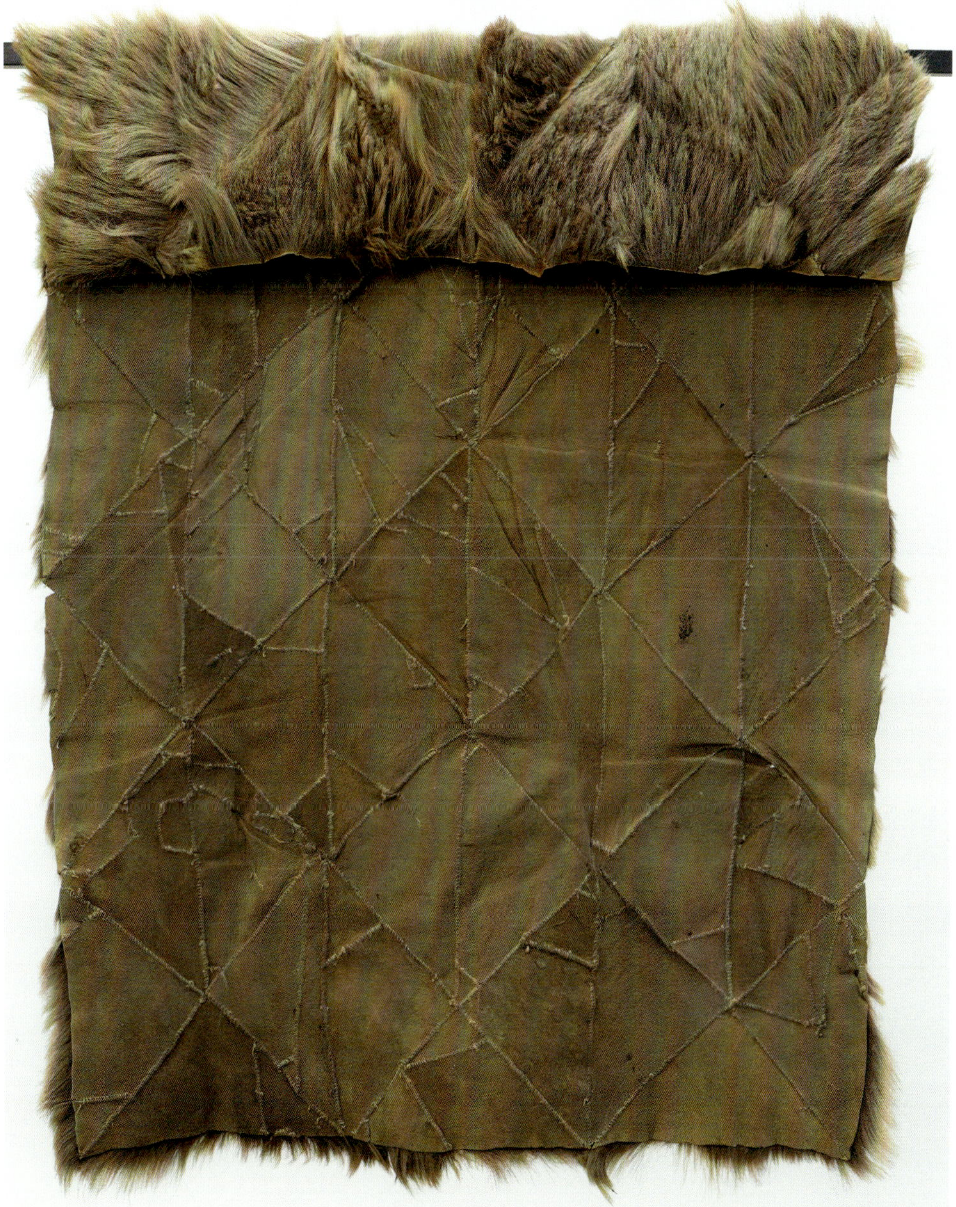

Caitlin Yardley
Peripheral Orbit (b)
2012
Steel and goatskin
75 3/16 x 96 1/16 x 17 11/16 in.
(191 x 244 x 45 cm)

This was a residency I did in about October last year with ACME, which is an organisation that runs several studio buildings in London. They do a lot of international residences, so I was supported through the Australian Government to do this with them following studying at Goldsmith's last year. They gave me a really large studio, which I worked in for two months. I had eight mentors and then I decided to put a show on at the end of the work. So I created an installation. *Peripheral Orbit* was the name of the entire installation.

Can you tell me a little bit about the title?

The show was built around this goatskin rug. I had a reference image I'd worked from, which was an image of a goat either stuck – it actually wasn't evident whether the goat was stuck in this fence or not – or just moving through it. I had been looking for goatskins and had been wanting to work with goat for a long time and eventually this one popped up, which is apparently a rug from the 1960s. Without even thinking I purchased it and then the show was built around that. It has this diamond stitching on the back – because it's quite detailed – that does not actually correlate with what happens on the front of the quilt.

It's hand-made?

Yes, and then I started to use those particular patterns on the paintings and also the title, which is this idea of the peripheral vision that goats have; they have those rectangular slits in their eyeballs.

That's where it's coming from, that's interesting.

They can see completely 320 degrees.

Oh, fantastic.

And the show was based on different bits of research. I was researching at the Freud Museum and a few other places; allowing things that were in my vision that may otherwise not be connected, to be connected, simply because I can see them at the same time and then unfold those things until there may be a material overlap, whether it's in a surface thing between the concrete and the surface of the painting, between steel and... You know, ways that I had already been working and the materials I was coming across as part of the research.

Caitlin Yardley was born in 1984 in Australia and lives and works in London. She holds an MA from Edith Cowan University, Perth (2007) and an MFA in Fine Art from Goldsmiths College, London (2012). Recent exhibitions include 'Changing direction after entering at an angle', Goldsmiths College, University of London (2012); 'Peripheral Orbit', Acme, International Residency Studio, London (2012) and 'An Intimate Distance', Venn Gallery Project Space, Perth, Australia (2011).

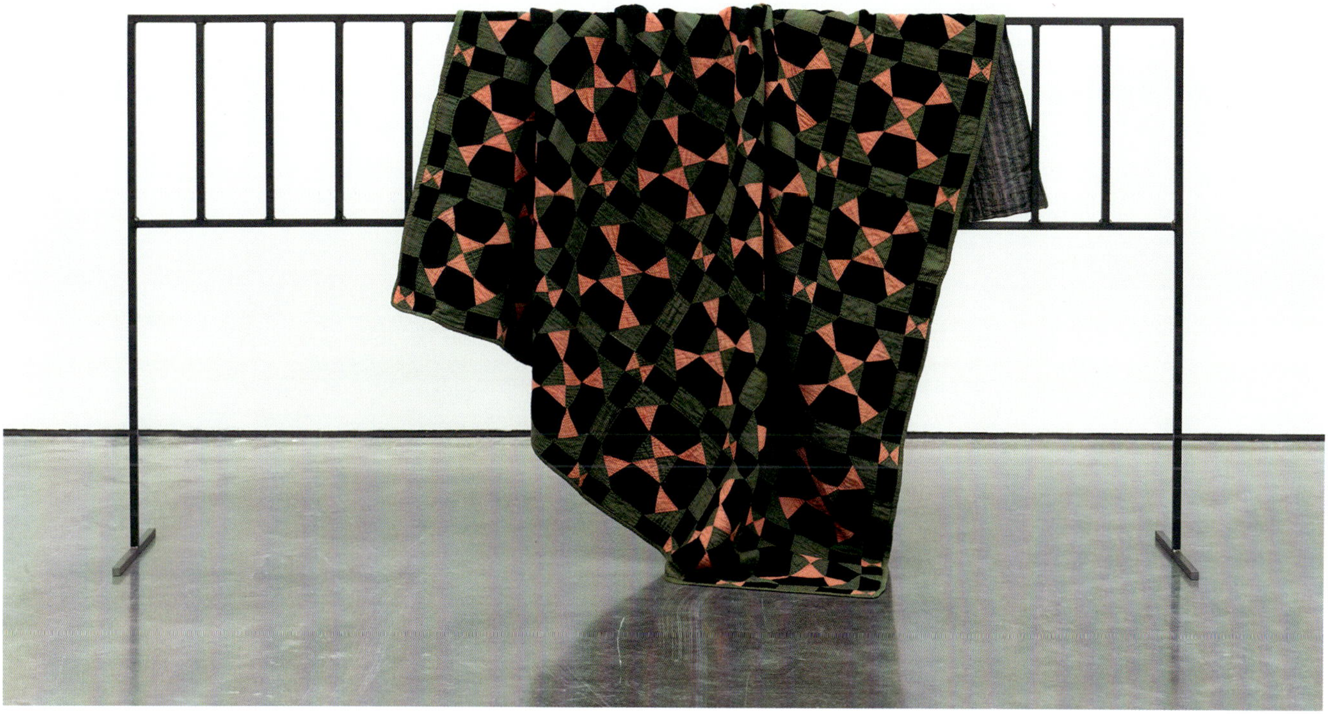

Caitlin Yardley
Black Refract (quilt)
2012
Steel and Amish quilt
43 5/16 x 87 3/8 x 15 3/4 in.
(110 x 222 x 40 cm)

Open Cube
Curated by Adriano Pedrosa

12 July – 21 September 2013
White Cube Mason's Yard

Edited and coordinated by Robin Kirsten
and Honey Luard
Artists interviews transcribed by
Robert Stephenson
Printed by Pureprint

Photography by Benjamin Westoby

Thank you to Jack W. Stauffacher for kindly
granting permission for us to base this
publication on his design for *Inside the White Cube: The Ideology of the Gallery Space* (The Lapis
Press, San Francisco 1986).

All the interviews published here are extracts
from transcripts of the original conversations.

978 1 906072 80 3

White Cube
25 – 26 Mason's Yard
St James's
London SW1Y 6BU

+44 (0)20 7930 5373
whitecube.com